FROM RED TO BLACK

A SHORT JOURNEY FROM DEBT TO LIBERTY
CHRIS GREENWOOD

DEDICATION

I dedicate this book, the principles, wisdom and ideas I've learned in the past 41 years of my life to my daughter London Grace Greenwood. Your mother and I have trail blazed the path, breaking the chains of debt off of our family tree and we pass these principles onto you.

"And you shall remember the LORD your God, for it is He who gives you power to get wealth, that He may establish His covenant which He swore to your fathers, as it is this day." Deuteronomy 8:18

FROM RED TO BLACK

A SHORT JOURNEY FROM DEBT TO LIBERTY

STAY DILIGENT!

PROVERBS 10:4

For information about special discount for bulk purchases, please contact us for special sales at: orders@manafest.com

Author: Chris Greenwood A.K.A Manafest

Written by Chris Greenwood & Teresa Stenson

Edited by Teresa Stenson & Mary Beth Conlee

Art Direction & Design by Melanie Greenwood

Manufactured in China

Manafest.com

FORWARD

From Red to Black should be compulsory reading for teenagers just starting their move into the challenges of adulthood, and also those adults who somehow have lost their way and are still struggling. They could use this book as a mentor. Chris has been through the pain of disappointments, broken promises, and exhausting schedules that would make others give up—yet his life is a magnificent success story.

As you read this book, it is all about reality! In each chapter there is a special message for you, so stop and meditate and underline that which applies to your own life, and use it. There is something else that must not be overlooked: Chris is a man of character, discipline, and ability, with a great love for his family. When I find a book as good and detailed as this, I buy some to give to my friends, and I strongly suggest you do the same. I give it a five star rating.

–Dr. Peter J. Daniels,
Founder and President,
World Centre for Entrepreneurial Studies, Australia

CONTENTS

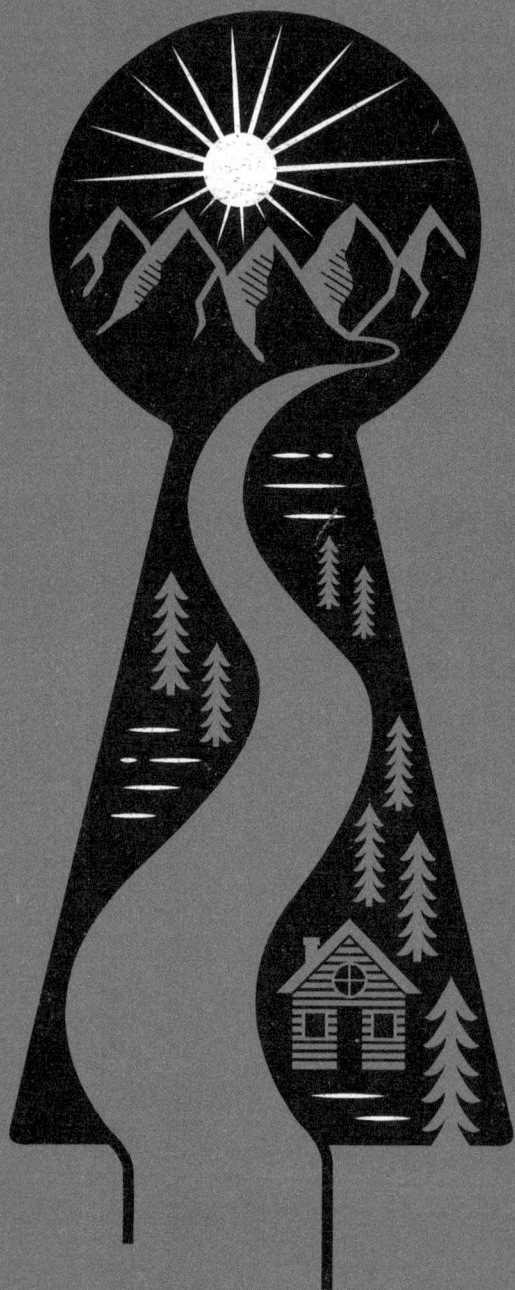

YOU ARE CALLED
TO LIVE LARGE

"One day, I'll have a house bigger than this," I told my mom. "Really? Good for you," she replied.

We were visiting a mansion owned by Mom's friends. I was seven years old, and already had visions of owning one just like it. I knew nothing about earning, investing, or keeping money, but the spark of creating wealth for my family had already been lit. As I humbly write this book to you from my private balcony overlooking a lake, watching a gorgeous sunset, I can tell you that having a vision for your life is powerful and not to be overlooked.

I was five when my father passed away, and in the years that followed I visited his wealthy sister's house for Christmas and birthdays. I vividly remember the luxury of the house as I walked through the front door and into my uncle's office. Sitting in his fancy leather chair, I'd look at the paintings on the wall while we listened to vinyl records on his souped-up stereo.

But it wasn't just the prestige and luxury I found so attractive. My Aunt and Uncle were some of the kindest and most generous people I encountered as a young child. I remember the sincere love I felt in their presence and the delicious meals we shared. And, of course, I remember how they gave the best presents. I wanted to have what they had, so that one day I could give what they gave.

SEEKING AN EDUCATION

When I was growing up, my parents told me, "Finish your dinner.

People in China and India are starving."

I tell my daughters, "Finish your homework.

People in India and China are starving for your job."

— Thomas Friedman

I lost my dad to suicide when I was five years old, and as such I was never taught anything about money or given a proper financial education. I believe when I was born again, the curse was taken off me spiritually not to take the path of suicide like my father.

Dad's parents weren't rich, and neither were Mom's. Aside from my brief visits to my wealthy Aunt's place, I didn't have exposure to people who knew about finance or how to achieve great wealth. If anything, I was told to put money in the bank to build interest. The bank is one of the worst places to keep your money because you only make 0-1% interest—but more on that later.

Not having a father triggered something in me to seek out successful men in all areas of my life. At church, I looked for Godly men who were successful in business and family. I had to step out of my comfort zone in my search for potential mentors. It was hard, because real men who are successful in both business and family are a rare breed.

I found most of these mentors in books, audio programs and online courses. I played their teachings over and over again in my car while traveling from city to city on tour. I've driven over four hours just to hear someone speak and flown over 17 hours to a different country to spend a day being coached 1-on-1. This type of personal development, and these in-person experiences, changed my life. Just being in the presence of entrepreneurs and thought leaders challenged me to grow and consider what my financial future could look like.

If you think education is expensive, try ignorance.

BECOMING A MASTER OF MONEY

When I started to break into the music industry my driving goal wasn't to become rich. I started writing songs because I wanted to share the message of Jesus with my friends. But when I quit my job to focus on my music, I found out it takes money to keep sharing a message. In fact, within a year of quitting my job, I was $30,000 in the hole. I can't begin to explain how crippling it was for me and my new wife to be that far in debt. The stress stunted my creative juices musically. However, it did force me to figure out how to make money with my music.

I learned through trial and error how to make money, pay off debt, and build wealth. And I have to say it's truly awesome to be able to share the many lessons I've learned with you now.

My hope is that this will open up your mind to some new ideas. I want you to forget the past and take a moment to really think—and feel—what being debt-free would be like.

How would it affect your life, your family, and the people around you? Too many people let their money control them instead of the other way around. I want to teach you how to be a good steward of money, and master it so it doesn't become a master over you.

My hope is after reading these pages, you will have a new outlook on wealth. My challenge to you is that you take up the mantel and commit to getting out of debt and becoming wealthy; not just so you can have more, but so you can give more and make a real impact on future generations.

ARE YOU BURYING YOUR TREASURE?

Some people are afraid of wealth because they don't understand money, or they're too scared to go into business. They seek the comfort and security of a job because they don't want to risk failure and embarrassment, but they are only denying their dreams and a life of unlimited potential. This self-sabotage brings to mind the steward who buried his wealth in Matthew 25:14.

In case you're not familiar with this story, let me paraphrase it. There was a man who gave three servants part of his treasure. To one he gave five bags of gold, to another he gave two, and to the last servant he gave one. When he returned from a trip he found two of the servants had doubled the riches they were given. But one servant was scared he would lose his new-found wealth, so he buried his gold and did nothing. The man was furious with him, calling him wicked and lazy for not even thinking to at least put it somewhere so that it could gain interest.

You might think you don't have talent, start-up money, or anything of value to offer, but the truth is, just by having access to the internet, you have an abundance of opportunities at your fingertips.

I believe being born into the luxury and abundance of the western world comes with a responsibility to act. We love to compare ourselves to people in our own country and say we are not wealthy, and there is no opportunity for us—but what about the rest of the world? Compared to 90% of the global population, anyone who lives in North America has unbelievable riches, freedom, and opportunity. So the question I need to ask is: Are you burying your treasure?

WRITING THIS BOOK WAS A STRETCH FOR ME

I've wanted to write a book on money for so long, but I kept putting it off because in truth I wasn't sure if I was ready for the criticism and attention that can come from tackling a topic that is taboo in many circles.

Another reason I held back on writing a book on money is because I doubted who would listen to me at my young age. I questioned my experience, and the fact I didn't study economics in college or university. However, I sought guidance from my millionaire mentors, who happen to be some of the greatest Christian business giants of this century. They said:

• "Chris, you are in a league of your own."

• "You are debt free, including the mortgage on your house, and have no consumer debt whatsoever."

• "You've traveled to over 22 countries and have gone into business, and you're winning!"

• "Many people speak from theory, but you have the opportunity to speak from experience and hard lessons learned."

Their feedback gave me the courage to go ahead and write this book. And now, I invite you to do the same: to stretch.

Sometimes you have to believe in someone else's

belief in you until your belief kicks in.

— Les Brown

STRETCHING INTO GREATNESS

You know you're called to something more. You know you're called to something great, but you let the fear of criticism or that voice of doubt stop you from pursuing it. I want to motivate you to think bigger. Les Brown says, "You can't shrink into greatness—you have to stretch."

If you want to be something you've never been before, you've got to do some things you've never done before… and that requires a mindset shift.

I know what it's like to lose sleep tossing and turning in your bed, thinking, how am I going to pay the bills this month? Or standing at the check-out line at the grocery store praying your card isn't declined. I've sat in church trying to worship God, trying to listen to the sermon to activate my faith. But instead, I've been worrying about how I could earn more money.

I remember taking my wife on tour with me to our first overseas show in Ireland. We went out for tea and coffee at this little café and had to discuss whether we could afford dessert or not. This was a serious conversation about ordering the sticky toffee pudding for seven more pounds. I'm happy to say we took the risk and enjoyed ourselves. There have been other times I've taken my wife out for dinner to a nice restaurant and I haven't been able to enjoy it for the guilt and worry over how much the bill was going to be. This is no way to live, and I got fed up living this way. If you are too, then I have two goals for you with this book.

#1 – I want to teach you how to get out of debt and be free from the chains that enslave so many by giving you a real understanding of money and how it works. I want you to experience financial freedom, enjoy your everyday life, and live your God-given dreams.

#2 – I want to equip you with time-tested principles, ideas and tools that I have personally used to become wealthy, keep that wealth, and transfer it to the next generation. I will show you how I did this without losing my family, getting divorced, or sacrificing my character or integrity—and while living a prosperous and joy-filled life.

Stop taking average advice from average people and
begin taking advice from extraordinary people.
– Stefan Aarnio

BEFORE WE CONTINUE: Are you ready to let go of any limiting beliefs you may have about money?

There are so many myths around money, and if we buy into them, they can really keep us stuck in the past—and the red. So before we dive deeper into the book, I'd like you to take a moment to consider if any of these limiting beliefs might be present in your attitude towards money. If they are, you can choose to challenge them and let them go.

#1. THE POORER YOU ARE, THE MORE SPIRITUAL YOU ARE

This is a belief that's quite common among the Christian community. In fact, many proudly wear the poverty mentality on their sleeve. This has never made sense to me, because it was a rich Christian businessman from my church who sponsored me to go to Bible camp one summer. My family couldn't afford it, and if not for this man's wealth and generosity I might have missed out on hearing the life-changing message of the Gospel. His gift impacted not only me, but millions around the globe whom my music has touched.

#2. MONEY IS EVIL

Money itself is neither good nor evil; it's just a tool. Think of it like fire: it's great in your stove and great for roasting marshmallows, but it also has the capacity to wreak havoc and cause immense damage. Every year people lose their homes to forest fires, and still we don't label fire itself as evil. Fire is neutral. It's a tool that can be used for the good or detriment of mankind. Both fire and money need to be respected and used with wisdom. Like fire, money is a tool that should be mastered to work for us.

#3. YOU CAN'T BE RICH AND BE A REAL ARTIST

When I first started out as a musician, I believed the term "starving artist" had some merit. I believed that if you were truly following your dreams and creating your art, your chances of making a living were slim. Only the 'chosen' rap and rock stars ever made any real money. The closer I rubbed shoulders with artists, the more I found it to be true: not many made money with their music, and those who did spent it frivolously. The wealth just didn't stick.

The truth is there are thousands of artists who aren't household names, yet they make an incredible living creating and performing music. Success in any industry requires more than talent. It takes resilience in heart, attitude, and relationships. It takes persistence and the courage to realize your dreams.

> *The starving artist waits to be noticed.*
> *The thriving artist cultivates patrons.*
> *– Jeff Goins, Real Artists Don't Starve*

I love that quote. To me, it says the thriving artist doesn't just wait around; he takes action and responsibility for his dreams. And that tenacity and willingness to grow applies to everyone: not just artists. I believe anyone who thrives in any industry requires a sense of urgency about their dream. That drive, along with a profound purpose, keeps them going when everyone else has given up.

Did any of these common money myths resonate with you? You might have your own set, inherited and passed down from your family or picked up from other people in your life. My advice is to let them go. Stop starving your visions and dreams, and your pockets will remain full. Add a sense of urgency and you're irrepressible.

CHAPTER 1
LIVING IN THE RED:
THE TRUTH ABOUT DEBT

The rich rule over the poor, and the borrower becomes the lender's slave.

— Proverbs 22:7

Living in the red has become a normal way of life for many in our society. If you were to look at the bank statements of the vast majority of people, you'd see they are living paycheck to paycheck, barely getting by. In fact, according to a study by Northwestern Mutual, in 2019 the average American was $29,800 in debt, not including their mortgage! Many are living in the red, or what the banks call overdraft: their bank account is in the negative even before credit cards or loans.

When I was growing up, being in debt wasn't the norm. It's interesting that many of us were wealthiest when we were teenagers; we had no debt and we had cash in the bank. I know that was true for me, because I wasn't allowed to buy anything unless I had the money to pay for it.

Big purchases, like a video camera to film skateboarding, required me to work my butt off all summer until I'd saved the money. Sure, I might have borrowed money from my mom sometimes, but 99% of the time, if I didn't have the money, I just didn't get whatever it was I wanted. I had to learn one of life's forgotten traits—patience—by learning to go without for a period of time. We have abandoned the concept of saving up to purchase an item. That's too bad, because we lose the feeling of satisfaction that comes when your hard work pays off and you finally reach your goal.

HERE'S THE SECRET TO CONTROLLING YOUR SPENDING

The secret to spending less is to pay with cash as often as you can. There is something about having all those crisp bills in your hand that brings a realization: this is real money. We can get detached from the reality of money when we only swipe our plastic cards, or look at numbers on a bank statement.

The fact is the banks want buying stuff to be as easy and painless as possible—until you get your credit card statement. Even then they try to keep you focused on paying the minimum payment. I know it's inconvenient, but just try buying stuff with cash as opposed to swiping your card. See if your behavior and your experience changes.

My wife told me that during her senior year of high school, there were credit companies in the hallways offering students credit cards. I couldn't believe it. Melanie didn't have a job or any way to pay a credit card off, but they gave her one, no questions asked. The next day she went to the mall to buy a whole bunch of stuff on her new credit card.

Wouldn't it be more effective if schools made personal finance a part of the curriculum? Imagine if, before a student graduated, they had a basic understanding of money, investing, and how to become wealthy. We don't give young people a driver's license to drive a car without training and passing a test. Yet we're ok giving a young person a credit card that can cripple them financially for years to come.

Schools teach us how to be good employees, but I think they could do a better job setting us up to win in the real world by providing us with a financial education.

WHY NOBODY CARES

Whether we realize it or not, the motivating factor behind a lot of what we buy comes down to our desire to impress others—even people we don't know, or like—just to keep up an image. Let me give you some perspective: Nobody cares. Nobody is thinking about you or what you look like or what you have. They don't have you on their minds; they have themselves on their minds. People are naturally extremely self-absorbed and most often they're dealing with their own daily challenges. Trust me, I'm one of them.

If one of my friends buys a new car, or clothes, or a house, I think about it for a second and decide whether or not I'm going to judge, envy, or congratulate them. After that, it's not on my mind because I don't really care.

I care about my own life. So why do we get into debt to impress people who really don't care? And if you think this only occurs in teenagers, you're wrong. Older people do it, just with more expensive purchases. Instead of the latest shoes, phone, or jacket, it's houses, boats, cars, and fancy vacations.

Don't buy things you can't afford with money you don't have

to impress people you don't like.

— Dave Ramsey

GOING IN THE RED

Debt is like a deep pit into which one may descend quickly
and where one may struggle vainly for many days.
– George Clason, The Richest Man in Babylon

MY FIRST DEBT

In 1998, I had just graduated from the Durham Business and Computer College, and I was sending resumes out to every job offer I saw in the newspapers and magazines. I was 20 years old. When a company called Insite invited me for an interview, I had to buy some khakis and a dress shirt quickly, because my wardrobe pretty much consisted of baggy jeans and shirts. I was ready for the skatepark, but not the office.

During the interview, I sat nervously shaking inside as Richard, the owner of the company, fired all kinds of technical questions at me. My palms were sweaty and my heart was beating a mile a minute, but somehow I kept my composure and convinced him I was the right guy for the job. I started off as a junior technician on $13.50 an hour answering tech support phone calls. I thought that was a ton of money at the time!

The problem was, work was a 30-minute drive away, and when I took the job I had just assumed my mom would lend me her car so I could make that daily journey. But she said no. I don't think I even looked into taking the bus or train, I just jumped right into buying a car—and right into debt. This was my first experience of living in the red.

I had no funds and no idea how to navigate the process of buying a car, but I had an Uncle who generously offered to lend me the money.

Together, Uncle Dave and I went to the Toyota dealership where we tried to negotiate a better deal by offering to pay with cash (Dave's cash, to be specific). It didn't work. How To Negotiate And Buy Your First Car After Graduating would have been an excellent course for a senior in High School. (I share my tips for buying a car—and paying it off—in Chapter Two.)

Uncle Dave borrowed the money from his bank at a good interest rate using a line of credit, and I paid him back at the exact same rate. He didn't even make a profit on me. My first car was a 1997 white Toyota Tercel with no air conditioning or power windows, but it got me from point A to point B.

Uncle Dave took a risk in lending such a huge sum to me, even though we're related. In fact, I'd say it was a risk especially because we're related. The truth is not everyone has the integrity to pay back a loan, and lending to a family member can lead to ruined relationships, even when the intentions are good. I'll never forget Dave looking me dead in the eyes, saying, "If you miss a payment, I'll break your legs." I believed him; Uncle Dave was a pretty intimidating guy.

The most valuable part of this experience came when Dave showed me all the numbers on the computer at his office, and gave me a bunch of different options on how to pay back the loan. He showed me the minimum payment—around $250 a month—and also how I could pay more if I wanted. I thought, why not $500 a month? Let's pay this sucker off as fast as we can.

We developed a system: I wrote a bunch of post-dated checks every four to six months, and he'd give me a phone call to remind me when he was about to deposit the last check. The total debt was around $13,000, which was a lot for a car back then. With hindsight, I could have gotten a great beater car for cheaper if I had better negotiation skills. I heard someone say the best time to buy a car is when you don't need one, so you can walk away from the deal. Otherwise, the salesman has you cornered, because he knows you need him more than he needs you.

This was my first introduction into debt, payment plans, and using other people's money. Thank God it worked out ok: I didn't default on the loan, and Dave didn't break my legs.

Integrity is doing the right thing, even when no one is watching.

– C.S Lewis

DEBT AND MARRIAGE

Melanie and I were googly-eyed in love when we got married. Neither of our parents could afford to pay for our wedding, so Melanie worked as a waitress after school to make extra cash; she actually paid for her dress with her tip money. We were the youngest amongst our friends to get married, and this was a blessing in disguise: because we hadn't been to many weddings yet we didn't have much to compare ours to, and we stayed pretty conservative with the budget.

We dated for five years, and during that time I became very successful as a network engineer, earning a salary of over $60,000—so we paid for our wedding with cash! On top of that, all the cash wedding gifts helped us set up our condo and our new life together.

One of the biggest dangers for newly married couples is to start their new life together under a pile of debt. That's one way to pop the honeymoon bubble: coming home and trying to figure out how to pay for everything at the same time as you're trying to learn how to live together. I suggest couples start their lives together by being conservative and not going crazy on the wedding, honeymoon, and new home.

Melanie and I have never split the bills or had "her money" and "his money." We were both transparent from the beginning. We shared our money, and, later, we shared our debt. I think it's a recipe for disaster when couples have private financial lives. We got into debt together, and we started to climb out of debt together.

You can't win together if you don't work together.
— Nick Saban

Once we were married, our first big debts were the mortgage on our 800-square-foot condo in Toronto, and Melanie's college debt. I was still making what I thought was good money at my computer job, and Melanie was working at her sister's spa, so managing the payments on those two debts was ok.

Eventually, Melanie got hired by a mutual fund broker in Toronto, and that's when we began to save again, with mutual funds. If you haven't come across this term before, a mutual fund is basically a collection of investments, such as stocks and bonds, owned by a group of investors and managed by a professional money manager. I personally do not recommend mutual funds. I think they're a rip-off. I learned from Robert Kiyosaki, author of Rich Dad, Poor Dad, that "the majority of a 401(k) retirement plan goes to the fund manager." Plus, they try to make as many trades as possible, because they make commissions on trades. I've never heard of anyone becoming a millionaire and creating real wealth through mutual funds.

The problem with mutual funds is you have to leave your money in there for a long period of time so it can grow tax free, and if you take it out, the government taxes you on it—except in the case of a first-time home buyer's plan. That's how we were able to purchase a condo when we got married: the "first-time home buyer's plan." It allowed us to take the money we had in mutual funds, as well as the funds my company contributed on my behalf, and put it towards the down payment on a home. What's special about this plan is that you can take the money out without the money being taxed—but you do have to pay it back.

THREE BAD DECISIONS ALL AT ONCE

Failing to plan is planning to fail.
– Credited to Benjamin Franklin

Next, I did three unwise things, all of which caused unnecessary debt and pain within our family: I quit my job to be a full-time musician, I put my career and finances in the hands of someone else, and I bought a $20,000 car using my credit line. It's painful to remember! But we live and learn—and hopefully there's a lesson or two in here for you.

#1. I QUIT MY JOB TO BE A FULL-TIME MUSICIAN WITHOUT A REAL PLAN.

I signed a record deal with stars in my eyes and assumed I would blow up with overnight success. I thought everything would just work out. Wrong! Nothing "just works out"; bills don't just pay themselves. Money doesn't just come in randomly because of my hopes and dreams.

I quit my $63,000-a-year job and jumped on the road without a proper budget. Every time I needed something, I just pulled out my credit card. I had very little experience in the music industry, and thought somehow my income would just be replaced.

When I signed the record deal, the record company immediately got 80% of all sales, so the only way I could make money was to tour. This forced me to go on the road 24/7, leaving my wife for months at a time to chase the dream.

What I should have done is built my music career up while working my day job, until the music income replaced my current job's income. I thought I'd be making music all day, swimming in creativity, but that wasn't the case. I was stressed out trying to make money from my music. I could have built my music career from home, played more strategic shows, and planned better tours, and I could have done it all without being so stressed out—because I'd still have a good income coming in. Many artists and entrepreneurs think you're only a real artist if you're doing what you love full-time, but that's not true. There is nothing wrong with funding your dream through your day job. I learned this lesson the hard way.

Instead, we roughed it for years, eating ramen noodles at home and the McDonald's dollar menu on the road. My wife paid the bills and supported us, thank God. She started back into modeling, which was super helpful because it paid well.

The first light of hope came from an unexpected source: the other side of the planet, in Japan, where I started selling 10,000 albums a week!

This breathed new life into my career and brought an unexpected cash influx into our much-needed home. It wasn't my constant touring that brought this money in—it was leveraging the songs I wrote by marketing them to a mass audience. I was hustling on the road playing to tens or hundreds, while the record label in Japan put me in front of millions without my even being there.

Just because you're working hard doesn't mean it's the right thing. Sometimes you have to step back and ask yourself if what you're doing is working. In my case, I call it grace. I don't believe in luck, but I do believe that the harder you work, the more opportunities tend to present themselves. But it's about doing the right kind of work.

When we stop and think what is the smartest, most effective way to do something, and focus on that, we get so much farther. All too often we rush into things without any plan, advice, or wisdom to guide us.

Looking back, I realize now what that part of my life was really about. I wanted to be a full-time artist, and I forced it to happen faster than it should have. Maybe I thought that if I stopped to think or ask for advice, I'd miss the opportunity altogether.

I know now I could have approached quitting my job and pursuing my music career more strategically and less painfully. But God is good and faithful, and I pushed through digging myself out of the debt.

We have books, stories, courses, and mentors so we can learn from their mistakes and avoid the pain. Pain is a good teacher, but I prefer to learn from others' experience.

Be anxious for nothing, but in everything by prayer and supplication,

with thanksgiving, let your requests be made known to God…

— Philippians 4:6-7

#2. AS A YOUNG, NAÏVE, HUNGRY MUSICIAN, I PUT MY CAREER AND FINANCES IN THE HANDS OF SOMEONE WHO WASN'T RICH OR SUCCESSFUL.

When you're learning from someone, you really need to ask yourself this question: if the person you're learning from isn't successful or rich, what makes you think they're going to help you become successful and rich? I teach business and finances because I've built a successful business with my wife for the last 10 years. I teach artists how to market their music and build a music career because that's what I've done successfully for the last 15 years.

Each person's destiny is not a matter of chance; it's matter of choice.

It's determined by what we say, what we do, and whom we trust.

— S. Truett Cathy, Founder of Chick-fil-A

When I quit my job, I hired a music manager to handle my business affairs. I made the mistake of choosing this person out of convenience, rather than because he was the best person for the job. This guy was supposed to help me generate more income through music performances, sales and other opportunities, but the only thing he helped me with was getting further into debt. Moreover, he discouraged all of my big dreams—while being the antithesis of ambition himself. I eventually fired him so I could take matters, and my fate, into my own hands instead of waiting for someone else to save me.

Sometimes we get so desperate for a dream that we flock to anyone who shows an ounce of interest. We think they're our financial or success savior and they'll make all of our dreams come true. Always check someone's track record and references. Look behind the curtain before you hand over your finances or trust someone with your dreams.

The first law of success is to maintain control.
— Peter J. Daniels

#3. I BORROWED $20,000 ON MY CREDIT LINE TO BUY A CAR RIGHT AS I QUIT MY JOB.

What a great plan. Not!

First of all, a car is not an asset, it's a liability. Assets put money in your pocket, and liabilities take money out. Cars take gas, need insurance, repairs, and monthly payments, which all cost money. Why I didn't just fix up the car I owned, I don't know. Maybe I thought it would break down on me, but it's no excuse to go into $20,000 dollars of debt! That was so stupid and unnecessary.

I could have bought a cheaper car, rented a car, or put a few thousand into fixing up my own car. Instead, I was on a spending rampage to force this dream to come true, and nothing was going to stop me.

Here are some questions you really need to ask yourself before making a purchasing decision:

• Is this the best way to solve the problem, or are there other ways to get it done?

• Is it the cheapest way?

• How can I do this without borrowing money?

• How can I be more creative?

Fortunately, the pressure of being in debt didn't drive my wife and I apart. Instead, it drove us closer together. She never blamed me for the dumb decisions I made, and I never blamed her. It gave us a common enemy to fight together.

Excessive debt will bring you sorrow, regret, and many sleepless nights.

— Manafest

FIGHTING A COMMON ENEMY

There is something extremely powerful when two or more people come into an agreement to chase a dream, or in this case, fight an enemy together. When my wife and I write down a plan, we pray over it and then act it out. Literally nothing is impossible for us.

Schedule a quiet time to sit down with your partner and calmly share some of the ideas in this book. Make a plan together to kick debt out of your life for good. If you're not married or don't have a partner, share your plans with a close friend or family member; someone who can keep you accountable on this new journey you're about to embark on.

If the devil roams around like a lion seeking whom he may destroy, then debt is like a wolf in sheep's clothing, fooling its prey by disguising itself as credit cards, delayed pain, and immediate gratification. Behind the tempting and glamorous façade are the chains that debt binds you with.

It's much more fun achieving things in life with a partner,

there's no question about it.

—Stefan Aarnio

This enemy is all around you. You're bombarded by thousands of messages a day via the media, by advertising, email marketing—even from your friends—to purchase things you don't really need.

For the love of yourself, your family, and your future, don't fall back into the debt trap that so easily enslaves. Instead, make a commitment that today, as you read this book, you will make it your top priority to get out of debt and become financially free. Say it out loud and write it down. "I am debt free!"

You don't have to be great to start, but you have to start to be great.

— Zig Ziglar

"EACH PERSON'S
DESTINY IS NOT A
MATTER OF CHANCE;
IT'S MATTER OF CHOICE.
IT'S DETERMINED BY
WHAT WE SAY, WHAT
WE DO, AND WHOM
WE TRUST."

— S. TRUETT CATHY
FOUNDER OF CHICK-FIL-A

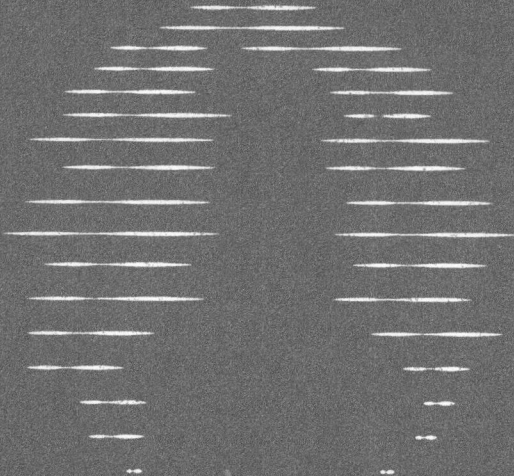

CHAPTER 2
HOW TO GET BACK IN THE BLACK

Debt is normal. Be weird.
— Mike Crofts

In the early days of our marriage, Melanie and I were hyper-focused on getting out of debt, throwing every extra cent we could find at it. I hungered for debt freedom amidst the sleepless nights, worried days, and past failures that put a halt to our dreams. My mind was stuck in a slump of misery from my debts, living paycheck to paycheck, thinking and praying for a way we could claw ourselves out of the mess.

I knew I was called to soar like an eagle and run with the giants I had always looked up to, but I hadn't made the full commitment to myself or my family. I let pride and ignorance lead, and like a sheep to the financial slaughter, I followed what everyone else was doing.

Wisdom was crying out, but it fell on deaf ears.

Working hard wasn't the problem. As I said in the previous chapter, you can work hard but get nowhere. The problem was, I wasn't working on the right tasks or asking the right questions.

I could no longer tolerate the pain and shame; something had to change. Then I heard a message preached by Peter J. Daniels that asked, "What is this mountain you want to climb? Do you just want a better job? Do you just want enough to get by on, or do you want to do something magnificent with your life?" I got the clarity I needed. I knew what I wanted: to be financially free so I could help others and make a difference.

I would like to take a moment to say something here: Making a difference, helping others, and now passing the ladder back down is very important to me—but despite the ladder reference, I don't see myself as elevated above anyone.

In fact, as you read this book I hope you see me as someone by your side, someone who wants the best for you. I have no judgment about you or your choices.

I know what it's like to feel lost and frustrated. I've had my moments in the sun, I've had my moments in the shade. I offer guidance from my experience, my beliefs, but mostly from my heart.

Next I'd like to share with you the three big revelations I had that set me on my road to freedom. I implemented the following steps into the way I approached my family's finances and they helped us get out of debt. I pray they will serve you as well as they did us.

Failure will never overtake me if my determination to succeed is strong enough.

– O.G Mandino

#1. WRITE OUT ALL YOUR DEBTS, SMALLEST TO LARGEST

Being honest with yourself is the first step to fixing any problem. I recommend you begin by writing all your debts down on paper or a computer spreadsheet, and then find the smallest one: that's the one you'll attack first. From this point on, put every extra dollar you can spare towards paying that debt off.

By doing this, you're no longer running away from your debt; you're taking action. And with persistent action, you'll pay off that first debt faster than you think. And it will feel great.

Once that's paid off, take the money that was going towards that first debt and put it towards the second one. Keep doing this until all your debts are paid off—and then focus your attention towards smashing your mortgage, if you have one.

The reason most people don't make progress is because they're not willing to trade the present for a greater future.

— Manafest

By starting with the smallest debt you'll experience the confidence of a quick win, and that will encourage you to keep moving. As you pay off each debt your momentum builds, your endurance increases, and you find it's easier to keep climbing the mountain.

You need grit and determination too: you want to engrain this new habit of channelling your extra money to your debts so it becomes automatic. After paying off that first debt, the "old you" might have said, "Hey I've got extra money now, let's go buy something," but instead, your new-found resilience ensures you use that extra money to pay off more debts. Soon you will have conquered the mountain and you'll be debt-free.

When I was paying off debt, I listed everything I owed in a spreadsheet, and updated it weekly, if not daily, so I could see my progress. I didn't care which debt had higher interest; I followed the advice I'm sharing here and focused from the smallest amount to the largest. Every time I made a little bit more money, I'd log in to my bank account and make a payment on my debt.

It's easy to get discouraged looking at the pile of debt in front of you, but let me remind you that all things are possible with God. Don't let regret or past failures stop you from chasing this dream. One passage of scripture that has always been a comfort to me in times of difficulty is Joel 2:20: "I will restore the years the locust has eaten." The reason we feel discouraged sometimes is because we lack clarity. But now you have a plan in front of you, so stop worrying about it. Just get to work.

There is only one way to eat an elephant: one bite at a time.

– Desmond Tutu

#2. SHORT-TERM PAIN FOR LONG-TERM GAIN

Being debt-free involves making certain lifestyle adjustments. For a short period of time, you need to live on less than you make, no matter the sacrifice. If you're willing to hunker down and go all in for a year or two, your future self will thank you for the rest of your life.

That's all we are talking about here: one or two years of hardcore debt-smashing so the rest of your life can be free. Imagine what life will be like three or four years from now, and what an impact that will have on your future—not to mention your kids' future.

The fact that you've read this far tells me you have it in you and you're an action taker.

Live like no one else, so later you can live and give like no one else.

— Dave Ramsey

There are always ways to cut expenses. My friend Shane Sams, founder of Flipped Lifestyle, cancelled his family's cable TV for a while so they could build their internet business. They downsized their house for a few years so they could save money to re-invest. He showed me the beautiful house they sold. Everyone thought they were nuts, but he made that small sacrifice then, and now they own the house of their dreams with a private lake.

Another buddy, Myron Golden, sold his TV and didn't buy another one until he was making $20,000 a month.

Melanie and I sold DVDs, old clothes, jewelry, and anything else we could to throw money at our debt. I went through my closets and basement and started listing items on eBay, Craigslist, and KiJiJi in Canada.

HOLD THE FRIES

Not eating out really hurt, because I enjoy my comfort food and the convenience of grabbing something to eat when I'm on the road. My daily Starbucks latte is one example. One $5 drink a day costs $150 a month, which is a good chunk to put towards a credit card payment. This was a hard transition for me because I drove an hour to work and an hour back every day. I learned to make tea before going to or leaving work.

The dimes add up to dollars, and at this point, every dollar counted. Any time I was about to purchase something, I thought to myself, do I really need this, or would I rather put it towards paying off debt? That may sound extreme, but sometimes you have to be fanatical for your freedom.

No one calls me crazy or fanatical now, especially when I cover the check at a restaurant. When I took my mom on an all-expenses paid trip to Texas, one night at dinner she said, "You don't look at the price on the menu, do you?" I said, "Not anymore, Mom, order whatever you want."

Start living on less and stop spending more than you make. Do a commando raid of your monthly expenses and see what else you can chop. When Melanie and I made the commitment to get out of debt, we looked at every single expense on our monthly bank statements. Then I started making phone calls. I called the insurance companies to negotiate better rates and cut policies that weren't really necessary.

When our mortgage was due for renewal, instead of just going with the same bank, we hired a mortgage broker, who shopped our mortgage around to different banks to get the best rate possible. Because we're self-employed, we weren't able to work with the bank that he brought to us, but we were able to take that exact rate and ask our bank to match it—and they did. This saved us thousands of dollars of interest while at the same time lowering our monthly payment. Boom!

The cool thing about hiring a mortgage broker is they only get paid when they close the deal with the bank, which pays a finder's fee upon closing. Even though his particular deal didn't go through, we gave our broker a gift certificate to thank him. He still helped us leverage a better rate with our current bank, and we were grateful.

Once we lowered our monthly mortgage payment, we used that extra $200 a month to—you guessed it—pay off more of our debts.

Some people want it to happen,

some people wish it would happen,

others make it happen.

— Michael Jordan

NINE WAYS TO LOWER EXPENSES

1. Stop paying for cable TV, or switch to a cheaper package that still has internet.

2. Limit how often you eat out, and take packed lunches to work.

3. Carpool to work a couple days a week.

4. If it's possible, sell or downsize your car, take the train or bus, even if it's just while you get back on your feet and out of debt.

5. Sell your house and downsize, like my friend Shane. Talk about delayed gratification that paid off big!

6. Melanie and I were able to cancel the mortgage insurance that was tacked on to our monthly payment. Call the bank and see if you can cut this from your monthly bill.

7. Cancel that gym, yoga, or other subscription you're not using. No amount is too small when you want to fire everything you've got at debt and invest in your future.

8. Call your credit card company and ask about lowering your interest rate. They'll take you seriously if you say you're considering switching to someone else and you'd like to transfer your balance over. You have to be tough with these guys.

9. For a short period of time, Melanie and I paid off our credit cards using the line of credit that was attached to our condo. This was at a much lower interest rate: 3-4% instead of the 18-24% credit card companies charge. It was a temporary plan so we weren't paying high interest charges. I don't recommend debt consolidation because that doesn't change your behavioral habits. Our goal here is to change your spending habits and attack your debt. If you have a clear plan to consolidate and then throw everything you can at the debt, that's fine. But if you're going to consolidate and then rack up more credit card debt, that's extremely unwise.

ACTION STEPS

I left some space on this page for you to write down some expenses you can cut. Make a list, pick up the phone, and start making calls. Cancel those online subscriptions today so you're not charged again.

EXPENSES I CAN CUT:

#3: INCREASE YOUR INCOME

Cutting expenses is great and helpful, but the real quantum leap in paying off debt comes when you increase your income.

When you do more than you're paid for,
eventually you'll be paid for more than you do.
– Zig Ziglar

How can you increase your income? This takes some brainstorming. Here are some prompts to get you started.

- Can you work extra hours?

- Could you get a second job at night or on the weekends?

- Can you learn a new skill? One of the best ways to increase your wealth is to develop special skills in an area that makes you money without requiring more of your time.

- Can your spouse start a side business?

- Are there friends you can call who might need some help?

- Consider taking an after-work job selling on commission, perhaps at a network marketing company. These companies tend to offer really great motivational sales training. I attended a USANA network marketing meeting with a friend so I could hear Darren Hardy speak, and his message alone was life-changing. These types of companies invest heavily in their people because they want you to do well.

YOUR IDEAS:

You might be considering starting an online business—this is an area I'll address more fully in Chapter Seven.

WHENEVER I'M TRYING TO EARN MORE MONEY, I THINK:

Who can I help?

What can I do that's valuable?

How can I provide more value to someone?

Pray, think, dream, and ideas will come to you. Remember: it's not about resources, but resourcefulness.

BANKRUPTCY: DOES IT HAVE TO BE TABOO?

I'd just like to take a moment to talk about the option of declaring bankruptcy. If you have several big debts and you've been struggling for a while, I'm sure this idea has crossed your mind already, but you might be put off by the stigma that surrounds it. I recently helped someone through this process and I have to say it was a real eye-opener for me: the bankruptcy trustee was incredibly helpful and the whole process was easy and smooth.

Think of it like this: bankruptcy laws are in place for a reason—so that we can take risks in business and still be supported if it doesn't all go to plan. The other thing to be aware of is if you're paying off a credit card with an interest rate of 12-18% (or higher) you're basically bonded to that debt for the foreseeable future. The interest is so high that even if you make a decent monthly payment you're barely putting a dent in what you owe, and often the debt just continues to increase. I'm not suggesting that filing for bankruptcy is the only option in a situation like this, but if you're paying $400-$500 a month in interest alone with no way to increase your income, it is something to consider.

My recommendation will always be that you first look to decrease your expenses, increase your income, and dig your way out of debt but if you seriously can't then bankruptcy is a legitimate way to start over if you need it. And if you couple it with an honest look at how you treat your finances along with a commitment to change any bad habits, you'll see it's not such a taboo route to take at all.

BECOME MORE

A few years ago I was given a great piece of business advice from a friend: increase your value as an individual so you can legitimately increase your prices.

As Jim Rohn said so eloquently, "If you want to have more, you have to become more."

How do you become more? One route is to learn a new skill by taking a course, or reading books to educate yourself in your field.

If you run a business, or you'd like to start one, do your research and see what your competitors are offering. Where are the gaps in the market? How can you expand your services? What makes you unique? Can you do more of that? Then consider how you can improve your marketing by positioning yourself as the best in your city, state, or country.

Never decrease your prices; know what you're worth, and increase your prices by adding more value.

Take your research to the next level by getting to know your customers, or potential customers. Find out what would make their life easier, what they struggle with, what they'd love to know, learn, or experience. Then work out how you can deliver that to them. These exact suggestions might not apply to your particular business, but hopefully you get the idea that this is about thinking outside of the box and shining light into any overlooked areas.

When I coach musicians, I give the following example: I could sell a poster as is, or I could sign it and number it. That immediately adds more value to the consumer without costing me much in time or effort.

Again, it's not about working harder—it's about working smarter. I know in the past I've had phases of working incredibly hard, often out-working my friends, and yet not moving the dial much. It wasn't until I got off autopilot and looked at what was actually working and what wasn't that I could make any real change. Then I started putting my energy into the things that really moved the dial, instead of wasting my time on frivolous activities that kept me stagnant. Change your focus from making more money to serving more people.

Serving more people makes the money come in.

– Robert Kiyosaki

RENT YOUR PLACE OUT

One of my musician friends was super savvy in earning extra money in unique ways. When we went on tour, he rented out his house via Airbnb. When he was home, he'd rent out one room; when he'd go on tour, he'd rent out two rooms. This was a great way for him to earn extra income and put all of his assets to work.

Some people do this when going on vacation: they rent their home while they're gone to help cover the costs of the vacation. The same friend would also purchase used guitars on Ebay and Craigslist and re-sell them while we were on the road.

I remember driving him to a house in Las Vegas before a show to buy $1500 worth of guitars from a stranger. He ended up selling those for over $2000 while on tour as an extra side hustle income. The opportunities are out there if you look for them.

I have another friend who offers accommodation to high school and college students who've come over to study from China. It gives the students a place to stay, and he's paid a pretty good fee for providing food and board and driving them to school each day. I know some families who got out of some serious debt by doing this for a short period of time. Plus, it helps the students.

Do you have a basement apartment you can rent out, or an extra parking space you don't use? Can you move into a place that has one so you can earn some extra income? When we rented out our condo we excluded the locker so we could rent that out separately to someone who needed extra space. We made an extra $700 a year for renting a tiny locker we weren't even using.

Never depend on a single income.

Make an investment to create a second source.

– Warren Buffet

CREATE YOUR WAY TO FREEDOM

Melanie and I are very artistic—she's a graphic designer and I'm a musician—so one of our go-to questions is always, "What can we create?"

I can perform for someone, feature on someone else's song, speak somewhere, or teach in exchange for money.

Melanie can create and sell a logo, an art print, a T-shirt, or another design. There's a website we use called Printful where you upload your designs to be printed on T-shirts, mugs, sweaters, posters, and pillows. Because it's a print on demand service we don't have to carry stock—all orders are produced and delivered to our customers by Printful.

It's a great way to experiment and innovate: you can take a cool slogan and toss it on a shirt, then post it on social media to see if it makes some sales. We did this one day for both my fans and Melanie's, with no cost except our time. We've made thousands of dollars this way with no risk in inventory at all. I'm going to get into more business ideas later, but this is one savvy way of thinking outside of the norm. A lot of people create shirts based on certain political or fashion trends, catching a wave of momentum and demand that's already there.

Think of your talents: what are you good at, or great at? I have a friend whose wife is an amazing cook, so she found a family who pays her to cook for them a couple times a week. Could you create an online tutorial, course, or coaching program, to share your talents with others? (We'll look at this more closely in Chapter Seven.)

How are you with a sewing machine? Several baby clothing brands start out in this same way: an inspired Mom gets creative and makes her kid an outfit, shares the photos on social media, realizes people love them and that there's a demand—and presto, a new business and a new brand is born.

My wife reminded me that during World War II, women showed great innovation and resilience by turning flour sacks into dresses and other items of clothing—to the extent that flour companies actually began printing more attractive designs on their sacks to entice customers. The possibilities are endless—you just have to put your creative hat on and brainstorm.

GIVE YOUR WAY OUT OF DEBT

And I will rebuke the devourer for your sakes,

So that He will not destroy the fruit of your ground,

Nor shall the vine fail to bear fruit for you in the field,

Says the Lord of hosts…

— Malachi 3:11

I am a very passionate tither and have been since I was a kid. At first, it took me a while to grasp the concept of tithing: giving back to God 10% of what is already His. I do this for a few reasons that I'd like to share with you.

1. I truly believe that God owns everything, including the beasts in the forests and the cattle on a thousand hills, as it says in Psalms 50:10. I'm only a steward of the goodness God has given me, so I'm just returning a portion of what is already His. This attitude makes me want to give back, but also affects how I manage what has been given to me.

2. Malachi 3:8-11 says, "Will a man rob God? Yet you say, in what way have we robbed You? "In tithes and offerings. You are cursed

with a curse, for you have robbed Me, even this whole nation. "Bring all the tithes into the storehouse that there may be food in My house. And try Me now in this," says the Lord of hosts, "If I will not open for you the windows of heaven and pour out for you such blessing that there will not be room enough to receive it."

My wife and I have tested tithing in our own lives over and over again. Every time we tithe, God blesses us even more. If you're reading this as a non-Christian and wondering how the concept of tithing can apply to you, there is an alternative. If the notion of 'giving back' is resonating with you, you might choose to give 10% of your income to charity. You can give to charity in a similar spirit that I give to my church: it's about making a contribution, being part of something. Instead of giving to God, when you give to charity, you may think of it as giving back to life. Instead of finding that God supports you in return—you may find that life supports you in return.

The more Melanie and I trusted God and also acted on our finances, the easier it got. I'm not saying to blindly tithe and not put in the work. That's where a lot of Christians misunderstand the concept. You have to change your actions, both in tithing and in how you currently manage your money and time.

It breaks my heart when I hear people say, "I just can't afford to tithe." I think to myself, You can't afford not to! Do you want the blessing of God in your life, or don't you? By not tithing, you're saying you can figure this thing out on your own. When you tithe and put God in first place with your finances, you're showing God you trust him and allowing him to come and intervene on your behalf.

The Bible says in Luke 6:38, "Give and it shall be given unto you, pressed down, shaken together, and running over." Be a cheerful giver, just like the Good Samaritan. God is my business partner, and I can't think of anyone better to have on my side!

GOOD DEBT VERSUS BAD DEBT

I'd like to introduce the idea of good debt and bad debt. Bad debt comes from credit cards, credit lines, car loans, vacations, and buying luxury items. So is there ever a legitimate reason to go into debt? Yes! With one caveat: when it results in increasing your income.

I believe debt can be used as a tool to create and build wealth, especially at the beginning of someone's journey to financial freedom. The opportunity to buy real estate, for example, and purchase an asset that makes you money, is extremely powerful.

Say you invest $20,000 of your money to buy a $100,000 property. You borrow $80,000 at a 3% rate, but you're making 10-12% on the money invested. What's so powerful about this is that you don't need $100,000 to buy a $100,000 property and receive all the benefits. You only need $20,000, and you can borrow the rest. What's also amazing is you get the appreciation of the house, not based on the $20,000 you invested, but the value of the $100,000 house you just purchased.

I also love the instant equity you can get if you buy a house that is undervalued from a motivated seller, especially if you then fix it up to increase its value. Lastly, I love the principal paydown you get from the renter who is paying off your mortgage by paying you rent each month. If you want to buy $100,000 worth of stocks, you need $100,000, because banks aren't in the business of lending people money to buy that type of investment. Why? Because it's risky, and not REAL like real estate. Banks want to make sure they get their money back if you can't pay the loan back!

However, money is seductive, and many people borrow too much and over-leverage themselves. They get to the point where they can't service the debt they've borrowed, meaning they can't pay the mortgage on the property. So be wise and prudent in making debt your friend, but in my personal experience, real estate has been one of the best investments my wife and I have ever made.

I love the quote from Harry J. Sonneborn in one of my favorite movies, The Founder. Speaking to Ray Croc of McDonald's, he says, "You don't seem to realize what business you're in. You're not in the burger business, you're in the real estate business. You build an empire by owning the land. What you ought to be doing is owning the land upon which that burger is cooked."

Real estate is at the core of almost every business,

and it's certainly at the core of most people's wealth.

To improve your business smarts, you need to know about real estate.

– Donald Trump

SPECIFIC PLANS FOR PAYING OFF CARS AND HOUSES

Now that you've started down the road of seriously dealing with your debt, you can consider some specific methods for particular types of debts. Let's start with the biggies: cars and houses.

PAY OFF THE CAR

I can still remember my wife and I skipping along the parking lot as we approached the door of the Scotia Bank. I looked over at her and said, "I can't believe we're actually paying off the car, this is freaking amazing."

If you recall, in the previous chapter I mentioned how I had zero experience in buying a car back when I was fresh out of college and Uncle Dave helped me out with that loan. Well, fast-forward a few years to when Melanie and I bought this car, the one we were about to pay off, and I have to admit I was still pretty clueless. I had no experience and no leverage. The best leverage when purchasing something is to pay cash, and we didn't even have a down payment.

Car dealers have a nose for this kind of thing, so when the guy we were trying to negotiate with shared a story about his manager asking people to leave if they tried to negotiate too hard to get a deal—we thought our only option was to borrow the money from the dealership through their lending process. We paid a high rate and definitely did not get a deal like we thought we were getting. But as the saying goes— we live and learn, and I'll share a couple of my tips on buying a car just down the page, all with the goal of making sure you get into as little debt as possible from the outset.

But if you're looking for something to kick-start the process of decreasing or even eliminating car debt altogether, think about selling your current car and downsizing. I know lots of families who've sold their BMW or Mercedes and they've still got a great car—and no monthly car payment to meet.

Another option to pay off your car faster is to negotiate a better interest rate. When I bought a car a few years ago, I was going to use financing through the car dealer until I realized I could get a much better rate at my bank. You might be able to tap into a credit line with your bank for 3% interest instead of 5% that you're currently paying through the dealership. The 2% saving you'll make on a $20,000 loan can go a long way, and it'll help you pay it off a lot faster. Just make sure there are no penalties for paying off the loan with the dealership before you make the move. Even if there are penalties make sure you do the math because you still might save more by switching.

Finally, when you get your next tax return rebate you might want to skip the vacation this time and pay off the car instead. Then maybe go on a less expensive road trip and celebrate your debt-free vehicle. When the time comes and you're buying your next car, here are some pointers based on the lessons I've learnt over the years:

#1. PAY CASH. Nothing puts you in a better negotiating position than paying cash for something and having the power to walk away. If they don't want to play ball, there's someone else who would love to take your money.

#2. BUY USED. I don't know of many other purchases where the item loses over 40% of its value as soon as you drive it off the lot.

There are so many great quality used cars that will save you thousands and thousands of dollars.

#3. GET SOMEONE ELSE TO PAY FOR IT. Ok—hear me out. When I buy my next car, I'm not paying for it—my renter is. What do I mean? Well, I'm going to purchase a rental property and use the income generated from it to buy my car. I want to make sure I'm always investing in assets that appreciate in value, not lose their value. Say you buy a $70,000 rental property that earns $650 a month in rental income. After mortgage, taxes, and management fees, you're left with a cashflow of $200. Then you have $200 you can put towards buying a car. One day, they will both be paid off, and now you have a car and a rental property instead of just a car that is worth less than what you paid for it.

> *The person who doesn't know where his next dollar is coming from*
>
> *usually doesn't know where his last dollar went.*
>
> *— Unknown*

THREE WAYS TO PAY OFF YOUR MORTGAGE

When Melanie and I made the decision to be debt-free—including our mortgage—we were relentless. When you're standing in front of the mountain you are trying to move, the first thing you have to do is believe you can do it. It sounds so simple, but if you don't believe you can do something, it's very hard to act on it.

We were like bulldogs, tearing into that mountain of debt chunk by chunk. There were three ways we started smashing the debt down on our mortgage—take a look and see which you can implement.

#1. PAY TWICE A MONTH

Check with your bank, and if you are on a monthly payment plan, see if you can switch to bi-weekly so you can pay it off quicker. This is what we did. It doesn't mean paying more; it means paying more often to pay less interest in the long run.

#2. DOUBLE UP

Next, we started to "double up" payments. Every other week, we paid extra onto our mortgage. So if our bi-weekly payment was $400, we could pay a minimum of $100 and maximum of $400 directly onto the principal amount. Talk to your bank and do the numbers yourself, but paying an extra $100 a month makes a huge difference in the years it takes to pay off your mortgage, saving thousands in interest payments.

#3. LUMP SUM PAYMENTS

Another powerful strategy is utilizing what the bank calls a lump sum payment. Depending on your mortgage contract, most lenders allow you to pay a one-time lump sum once a year equal to 10% of the principal or your original mortgage. For example, if you had a $200,000 mortgage and you wanted to make a lump sum, you could pay as much as $20,000 in additional principal payments per year for the life of the mortgage.

It gets exciting when you see the principal start to get lower and lower. What's even more exciting is when you see that the majority of your monthly payment is going towards the principal instead of interest. This is where momentum really starts to build, like a wave swelling to its maximum peak. I remember thinking to myself, *Every* dollar I save, I can smash at the mortgage. I didn't care how small the amount was. I was determined to throw everything I had at this thing.

I was getting used to calling the bank and asking them to transfer a lump sum payment or set up double up payments, and it was always smooth sailing—until the day I called to say I wanted to make a final payment on my mortgage.

The representative's tone changed completely. She did her level best to dissuade me, saying I didn't have any more lump sum payments available, and that I'd be charged a fee. I said that was fine, and I wanted to proceed anyway.

"Are you sure? Because you will be charged a fee." She was either really concerned about me having to pay that fee, or she really didn't want me to make that final payment.

"Yes, please go ahead and pay it off with the money in my account." I was put on hold. After five minutes she finally came back and said she could make the payment, and I'd be charged a small fee for closing the mortgage. I think it was called a discharge fee, which was nothing compared to the amount of interest we'd pay otherwise. I just wanted to be finished with it.

I can't begin to tell you the amazing feeling of paying off the mortgage. We had already become free of consumer debt from credit cards and car loans, but to pay off our condo felt like a dream. Walking around our debt-free home, on debt-free carpets, cooking in our debt-free kitchen, sitting on our debt-free couches, we celebrated.

CELEBRATE YOUR WINS

Statistically, divorce and money problems are linked, and when you are conquering a mountain, you can get tired. Sometimes you need to rest on a peak or lay your head down, because you feel like it's been uphill the whole way.

This isn't the time to look up and get discouraged with how much farther you have to go. Now's the time to look back and see how far you've come! Celebrate with your significant other and go out for dinner. Do a little splurge. Don't go crazy or borrow money to do it, but something to pat each other on the back goes a long way. This is something I wish I'd done more often, because life isn't just about conquering mountains and achieving goal after goal. It's interesting to me that once I paid off our debts, I celebrated for a short while, and then it was on to the next mountain.

Enjoy the journey. Make it a game as opposed to a stress, and you'll have a lot more fun. Life will be filled with more joy. You can enjoy a life that is purpose-filled, debt-free, and you can achieve your dreams at the same time!

MIND YOUR MOTIVATION

You can use all the techniques in the world and live close to the bone, but unless you want to go right back into debt, you have to keep your "why"—your motivation to stay free—uppermost in your mind. The seduction of money and how easily you can borrow on credit in our culture is so tempting, and of course we so often fall for it. This reminds me of the famous question, "How much is enough?" The answer: "Just a little bit more."

As a dog returns to his own vomit, so a fool repeats his folly.

— Proverbs 26:11

Being content—knowing how much is enough—is so powerful. It not only stops you from borrowing just to fit in or to keep up with our culture, but it also allows you to appreciate what you've got. There'll always be someone with a nicer car or bigger house, but who cares? If you, like the majority of my audience, live in North America you're in the top 5% of the richest people in the world. Do you really need to compare yourself to those who have more?

Let's look at some guidelines for our relationship with debt to ensure we don't slide back into our old ways.

PAY THE PRICE NOW SO YOU CAN PAY ANY PRICE LATER

When my wife and I got married, we didn't buy the latest furniture. We didn't have a fancy car or eat out at expensive restaurants. Our focus was always on putting our money back into my music company, Manafest Productions, or Melanie's art business, Vision City. There were times we thought, When are we going to get our chance? When are we going to get the nice toys and go on the vacations?

After 14 years of marriage, we just bought our first nice used truck. We actually bought a truck a few years before that was nice, but we returned it after a month to put the money on our mortgage, and got a cheap van for touring instead.

For years we built our businesses, invested in real estate and our education, and got coached by some of the greatest minds in the 21st century. We delayed gratification so one day we would be in a position to do all these fancy things. For years we lived below our means so we could save and have our money working for us. Honestly, it's only been in the last two years we've felt like we could enjoy some of the fruits of our labor.

People say they want wealth, or to build a business and make a huge impact, but there is always an exchange that takes place. There were many nights we both had to work late and couldn't hang out with friends. I didn't hang out with a lot of friends after church or go out after a concert, because I was preoccupied with the goal and calling placed on my life. At times it was lonely being the leader of my band and my family without having anyone I could relate to, but I pressed on towards my goal.

I sacrificed seeing my friends when I decided to go on tour for months at a time. Then there were periods where I couldn't see Melanie for six weeks at a time, which was extremely hard. But we had the conversation ahead of time, prayed about it, and decided we were willing to go without each other for a short period, so that later, we'd have the flexibility to work or hang out together whenever and wherever we wanted.

To get a business or any great venture off the ground takes sacrifice. With wealth and leadership comes loneliness. You have to be able to handle the pressure and loneliness and be willing to trade your life for an awesome dream.

SOME PEOPLE ASK ME IF IT WAS WORTH IT

I have to say an enthusiastic "Yes!" It was worth it for us because we know the lives we've changed. We know the impact we've had around the world to get this message of hope and Jesus's love to people who might not have heard it otherwise. It also made us closer because we were working on our dream together. Many husbands and wives are not on the same page and chase their dreams apart from one another. We always worked on our dreams together.

KNOW YOUR "WHY"

There is a difference between a career and a calling.
Career is based on the amount of compensation.
A calling doesn't care what the pay is.
— Brendon Burchard

It takes hard work to get out of debt, so I'd like to come back to the importance of knowing your "why." Money only motivates you so much—there has to be something bigger you're fighting for.

I didn't get into music to make money. I got into music to share the gospel of Jesus. I learned how to monetize the music so I could sustain the message.

The reason so many artists, creatives, and preachers quit is because they don't know how to create an automated income that allows them to continue doing what they love. The majority quit and get a job, and then can't put nearly as much work or effort into the things they really love because they have to pay the bills.

We all have the same 24 hours each day. The difference is what you do with those 24 hours. I don't believe life should be all about work 24/7; that's not what I'm saying. It's extremely important to rest and take those family vacations so you don't burn out—which I have experienced on occasion.

One year, I played over 150 shows, traveling to multiple countries, flying home for a day to see my wife only to pack to leave the next day. I sat chatting with her the night before I had to fly out again, eating a grapefruit, and I accidently spilled some on our new leather couch.

As she picked up a cloth to wipe it up, for some reason, as I said I was sorry, I just started bawling my eyes out. The tears just poured and poured, and I picked up the phone, called the promoter of the next show, and cancelled it. Then I re-scheduled my flight. I can't tell you the peace, comfort, and joy that came over both of us. Not only did my body and mind need rest, but my marriage needed nurturing.

It would have been great if I had set better scheduling boundaries in the first place. I needed to reconnect to my wife and my purpose, because if my fuel tank is empty, I have nothing left to give to other people.

At the end of the day, I am in control of my calendar and my yearly schedule. I am the architect of my life, and I can design it however I want. It's ok to say no, pause, and rest.

I've discovered that life is made up of different seasons and change is inevitable. Recently, for the first time in 18 years, I emailed my booking agent to say I'm not doing any shows this year. It was scary and completely out of the norm because touring was my life—but I had entered a new season. This didn't come as too much of a shock to my agent because I had already pulled back from touring gradually. Don't be afraid to tell people no, and remember: you are responsible for your own schedule.

Don't wait for everything to be perfect before you decide to enjoy your life.

— Joyce Meyer

PREPARE FOR THE NEXT DEPRESSION

There's one more motivation for staying out of debt, and that's the future. I believe without doubt that another recession and depression is coming very soon.

It's going to be bigger than the financial crash of 2007 and, in my opinion, it will last longer. At the time of writing (late 2020) the world's economy is beginning to piece itself back together after the global COVID-19 pandemic.

It's still early days and there's a lot of uncertainty about how we can get back to 'normal'—or even what that new normal will look like. But considering the impact the virus has had on the economy, along with the fact that governments across the world have been creating money at an astounding rate, I can't help but think this could spark the next recession or depression.

This makes it more important than ever to invest in assets— something that we'll look more closely at in the following chapter. The truth is, most people aren't prepared for the realities of a major economic downturn.

Peter J. Daniels said to me, "The one thing we learn from history is, we don't learn from history." It doesn't take a Ph.D. to see that the world runs in cycles, and similar signs show before each calamity, if we just take the time to look. It's not a matter of if there is a recession, depression, or downturn in the market, but when. So what does a person do if they know something of this magnitude of disaster is coming? I suggest the following five-step strategy.

#1 – Get out of debt as fast as you can

#2 – Don't go back into debt

#3 – Increase your income and lower your expenses

#4 – Diversify your assets globally; don't keep them all in one country or jurisdiction

#5 – Help your family do the same

This is why it's so important to lean on the conservative side and build wealth at a steady pace.

Wealth from get-rich-quick schemes quickly disappears;

wealth from hard work grows over time.

— Proverbs 13:11 (NLT)

BACK IN THE BLACK

A woman said to a friend, "I'm going to go back to law school." Her friend said, "But that's going to take five years!" She responded, "Well, five years are going to come and go anyway. I might as well have my law degree at the end of them."

That spoke to me. Time is going to come and go anyway. Why not be out of debt in five years or less? Life goes by so fast. You can put the time and effort in now and reap the rewards in five years, or reap the negative consequences.

Don't underestimate what you can get done in one to three years if you start working towards your goal today. I've wanted to write this book for many years, but it was when I set a deadline and a date, and started to work at it, that it finally got done. What gets scheduled gets accomplished—so put your goal on your calendar.

Write down the amount of debt you want to pay off or the amount you want to save. Post it on your wall, fridge, or somewhere else visible to remind you. Then start taking the steps towards achieving it.

*Most people overestimate what they can accomplish in a year
and underestimate what they can achieve in a decade!*

— Tony Robbins

"SOME PEOPLE
WANT IT TO
HAPPEN,
SOME PEOPLE
WISH IT WOULD
HAPPEN, OTHERS
MAKE IT HAPPEN."

— MICHAEL JORDAN

CHAPTER 3

GOOD HABITS OF THE RICH AND BAD HABITS OF THE POOR

If you want to be happy, study happiness.

If you want to be rich, study rich people.

– Jim Rohn

First, before we dive into this chapter, it must be said that I recognize there are a lot of reasons why people find themselves living in poverty, and many of those reasons are out of their control.

Though I'm writing a chapter here on the different habits of the rich and the poor, I have no desire to make judgments about anyone's circumstances or lifestyle choices. I write this book from a place of love and respect for my fellow humans, with the sole intention to empower and inspire.

Often, when we're busy living our day-to-day lives, there's a tendency to go on autopilot. We might find ourselves in similar daily routines to the people who raised us, or as our friends, or as our co-workers. Over the course of our lives, we pick up habits and belief systems without realizing that they could be keeping us limited. It's only when a light is cast on those limited ways of thinking or being that our minds open up to change. This is exactly how it happened for me.

I didn't start reading or studying anything about the rich, their habits, or how money worked until I was in my early twenties. By then, I was already in a lot of debt. I knew the basics: going into debt was bad, and having money was good—but I had no idea how to get out of my current situation or who had the road map to this financial promised land.

My cousin Dave Mischuk (whom I have to thank for many things) gave Melanie and I a wedding gift: a book called Rich Dad, Poor Dad, by Robert Kiyosaki. In it, he wrote, "To Chris & Melanie, this is the second-best book I've ever read besides the Bible."

Despite such an endorsement, I didn't open the book until years later. Like most 24-year-olds, I thought I already knew everything there was to know, and besides—I was super focused on my dream of becoming a rock star.

But we were in a massive amount of debt, and I was struggling to figure out how this money thing actually worked. I saw our house mortgage like a game: we were trying to pay it off as fast as we could, but as the mortgage went down, the credit line went up. We were running on a treadmill: going nowhere.

I challenge you to make it a priority to study the rich and implement their habits in your life—and I invite you to discover the habits of poor people, and stop doing what they do. Here are some habits of both groups that I've learned and observed.

FIVE HABITS OF THE RICH

#1: THE RICH INVEST IN ASSETS

I vividly remember the night I started to read Rich Dad, Poor Dad. Every few minutes I'd shout, "Oh my gosh!" "I can't believe this!" "Wow. I had no idea."

I suddenly understood clearly why I was broke and it boiled down to this: the rich invest in assets—things of value that make them money, as opposed to the poor, who invest in liabilities or consumer products that only take money out of their pockets. It was a real lightbulb moment for me.

Assets make you money. Examples include rental properties, businesses, paper assets, song and book royalties, online courses.

Liabilities take money out of your pocket every month. Examples include cars, houses, vacations, jewelry, shoes, alcohol.

Use the space on the next page to list your assets and liabilities. If you don't yet have any assets, get creative and brainstorm what you'd like to see in that column.

ASSETS	LIABILITIES

Another name for assets is income streams, and your goal should be to have multiple streams of income—not just from your job. You could lose your job at any time, and if you don't have multiple flows of income, you're putting yourself and your family at risk. The average millionaire has multiple sources of income.

#2: THE RICH USE THEIR TIME TO LEARN

Formal education will make you a living;

self-education will make you a fortune.

— Jim Rohn

Wealthy people are constant readers and learners. In fact, in almost every interview I've read or watched with a billionaire, the importance of reading is mentioned. From Mark Zuckerberg to Elon Musk to Bill Gates—they all credit the incredible power of books as a key component of their success. Gates himself has said multiple times that he reads 50 books a year, and a few years ago Zuckerberg set himself the challenge to read a book every two weeks for a whole year. Honestly, do a quick Google search for How many books do wealthy people read and you'll find thousands of articles championing what is a fairly straightforward and simple habit.

I'm a big advocate for reading myself: I read somewhere between 20-40 books a year, including audio books that I download for long walks. Reading expands the mind like almost nothing else. Wealthy people are always in a state of growth and willingness to learn— whatever their age.

Compare that to the fact that most people who graduate from college see that as the end of their education. I believe self-education should be a normal part of life, and it goes beyond reading:

I've spent more money on seminars, conferences, courses, and books than I did on my college classes! I'm always looking for that one new idea or edge that keeps me sharp. My friend Myron Golden said it well in his book, The Trash Man to the Cashman, "The difference between rich people and poor people is, poor people entertain themselves, while rich people educate themselves."

Can I challenge you to not watch Netflix and stay off social media for a few nights this week? Or even every night this week? Instead, read a book, take a course, or learn a skill that could help you increase your income and your financial education.

Cancel the Netflix account until you're financially free. Delete your Instagram account—unless you're using it to build a personal brand that's going to earn you an income one day.

Set yourself up for success by eliminating timewasters, because time is the most precious asset you own.

MAKE WAITING TIME LEARNING TIME

My car doesn't move unless I have two types of fuel: gasoline for the car and education for my mind. Even when I go for walks, work out, or do household chores, I have my wireless earbuds in and a podcast or inspirational message playing.

I've spent a huge portion of my life touring around the globe on tour buses, in cars and on planes, sometimes traveling five to eight hours a day only to be on stage for one hour. Most of my fellow musicians would be bored out of their minds and couldn't wait to get to the show. Not me! I'd take multiple books and turn the tour van or airplane into a mobile university.

I've visited hundreds of cities across the world, and whenever I get a chance I go into the local thrift shop or used bookstore. I love searching through the personal development, motivational, and business sections, looking for a gem for a buck. The way I see it is I'll happily trade a few dollars in exchange for a book that inspires an idea that might be worth a hundred to a thousand times more.

This is exactly how I first found one of my favorite books: Think and Grow Rich by Napoleon Hill. I was in New Zealand, killing time before a show, when I found myself in a little book shop and that title Think and Grow Rich just pulled me right in.

I scanned the pages and knew I'd found a gem. I love this line: "One of the most common causes of failure is the habit of quitting when one is overtaken by temporary defeat." I'm sure I'll share more wise words from Napoleon Hill before the end of this book!

I'm always in search of good inspirational material because in the music business—and in life in general—we're faced with so much rejection and negativity. I glean books for inspiration for songs, business ideas and investment tips. Books are incredible tools when you think about it: someone is teaching you everything they've learned on their journey, and you can apply those lessons to your life in a few days. I love the Sam Levenson quote, "Learn from other people's mistakes. Life is too short to make them all yourself."

People often ask, "What is your most precious asset?" Many say it's your earning ability.

My answer is time. You can always earn more money, but you can't create one more second of time. Be mindful about how you choose to invest your time. As my hero, Peter J. Daniels, says, "Never allow waiting time to be wasted time."

I love how he taught this point during a seminar. In front of the audience, Peter lit a fire in a metal can, and started dropping twenty-dollar bills into it. The audience gasped, some even shouting out "Stop!" But his point was crystal clear: that's exactly what we do when we treat our time like a cheap commodity—we let it go up in flames along with our dreams.

Most people will gladly spend more money on haircuts each year than on inspirational business books that could totally change their life! I'm not against great haircuts or expensive fashion, but if you're broke, you need to get your money situation fixed before you pay hundreds to get your hair fixed.

Learn to control your time, invest your time, and use it to your advantage. It's the most powerful tool you have.

Some people get defensive when I suggest reading books. Common pushbacks I've heard are: "All that stuff in there is just common sense," to which I say, "Sure, but common sense isn't always common practice." (I might also ask why, if it's just common sense, they're broke and having to borrow money.)

The other excuse is, "I don't have time to read." They don't have time to read? One look at their Netflix account and Instagram history might give a clue to where they're spending their time. Others tell me they hate reading—so I say get an account with Audible.com and listen to books. Just please stop making excuses.

Here's a good one: "I'm tired by the end of the day and I just want to veg out for a while." I get tired too, and there's nothing wrong with a little relaxation with TV, but what about watching something inspirational? When I choose to watch something inspiring, it energizes me.

A comfort zone is a beautiful place, but nothing ever grows there.

— Unknown

EDUCATION. IS COLLEGE A GOOD INVESTMENT?

Rich people learn constantly. But is going to college a good way to begin a career that will lead to wealth? According to Collegedata. com, in 2019-2020, the average "net price" for tuition, fees, room and board was approximately $15,400 at public institutions and $27,400 at private colleges.

There's no way I could have afforded that coming out of high school, and my mom wasn't in a position to help me out financially. In fact, that's probably why I can't ever remember having a serious conversation about going to college.

My people perish for a lack of knowledge.

— Hosea 4:6

At the end of high school, all my friends were applying to colleges and universities with plans to get degrees and find a corporate job in the field of their choice. I, on the other hand, had plans to become a professional skateboarder while working part-time. If it weren't for my close friend Bruce, who owned a computer college and suggested I further my education in computers, I would have missed out on a huge opportunity. This was a very specialized and focused college training program that only lasted eight months.

The cost was $8,000, but Bruce negotiated a deal with me: he'd waive the course fees in return for me working as the janitor and tutoring other students. What a great trade—I got this education practically for free, with my only costs being my books, and my time when I stayed after class to clean and to help my fellow students learn. I couldn't have asked for a better deal.

What I like about community college is that it's specialized and focused on developing a specific skill. I wasn't forced to take extra classes that had nothing to do with my career, as is often the case in other colleges and universities. It frustrates me to hear of students who are studying business in college and are obligated to take non-related general education courses that have nothing to do with their degree.

My wife was forced to take a nutrition course when she was earning a graphic design diploma. It's not only inefficient, but a huge waste of time.

Many students take out a loan to pay for college, which is extremely different than taking out a loan for a mortgage. With a mortgage loan, if you can't pay the bill, you can walk away from it and lose the house—which of course isn't great—but a college loan is with you for life until it's paid off. Plus, the interest on the loan continues to grow, compounding the debt (and keeping millions of students enslaved).

Sadly, countless college students who graduate can't even get a job with the degree they just spent hundreds of thousands of dollars on, and they often end up getting the same job they could have applied for before college. Now they're forced to do a job in a non-related field to pay off the school loan. Ironically, university students with fancy degrees often end up working for college dropouts who became entrepreneurs.

Before you think about going to college, ask yourself if it's really going to give you the skills and ability to get your desired job. I see so many students go to college just because of pressure from family, friends, and guidance counselors who suggest it's the only way.

Going to college or university is a massive decision. Who says you have to make the decision so abruptly? Especially when it means going into debt. I remember sitting down with Melanie when we were dating and having a long discussion about it. She recognized that college was a life-changing choice, and she made sure that's what she really wanted.

When she borrowed the money to go, she worked her tail off applying for scholarships and grants to help pay it off. Once she graduated and we got married, we were super focused to pay it off as fast as possible.

The college loan was through the Ontario Student Assistance Program, and they only asked for a minimum payment, which would keep us in debt longer. We chose to pay $400 a month to pay it off quicker and save the interest.

Personally, I would never go to college or university because I can take online courses that have more up-to-date information and allow me to get the skills I need faster. Then I can get to work making money. I prefer to learn from the person who is not just teaching from a textbook, but living it out.

Those who have focused, specialized skills in an area are generally paid the most in any given field—not because they're pretty good at a bunch of things, but because they're amazing at one. Nobody celebrates the jack-of-all-trades who is pretty good at everything, but we do hear about the guy or gal who is known for being the best.

People pay $60,000 with outrageous interest rates to attend a college or university, all the while learning from people that make $40,000 a year, so they can maybe, in four years, get a job that pays $50,000 per year.

– Dan Henry

#3: THE RICH HAVE A VISION OF THE FUTURE

Rich people set goals every year so they can keep track of their progress. This keeps them focused and working towards something instead of staying stagnant. I've heard it said that if you don't have a five-year goal, then you don't plan on being around in five years.

I was walking down the streets of the city of Vancouver with my first music business coach when he asked me a very penetrating question: "Where do you see yourself in five years?" At the time, I didn't have an answer, but you better believe I do now: not just a financial goal, but goals for my family and my health.

#4: THE RICH SAVE MONEY

The rich pay themselves first before paying everyone else. They do that by taking the first 10-20% of their monthly income and investing it into an asset.

The rich carry financial reserves so when there's an economic downturn, their wealth is protected. The poor live paycheck to paycheck: one unexpected expense, and they're totally wiped out. Your goal should be to have cash reserves that would last you six to twelve months in case a health problem or some unforeseen circumstance catches you off guard.

Les Brown says, "You can never have enough money for the unexpected." Build up your reserve fund over time.

#5: THE RICH SPEND LESS THEN THEY MAKE

Rule #1: Never lose money. Rule # 2: Never forget rule #1.

— Warren Buffet

I log into my bank accounts every day to check the status of things—not because I'm worried, but because I like to keep a pulse on my business. We spend a lot of money advertising Manafest and Smart Music Business, so I always check to see how they are performing. I wake up to see if I made money, broke even, or started out at a loss, and adjust accordingly.

Some of my friends think this is a bit excessive, but I like to measure each day to make sure my expenses don't exceed my income. I have a friend who works at a credit card company and he sometimes spends time with people who don't understand why their bill is so high. He goes through each item line by line until finally they say "Oh, ok, I forgot about that."

Have you ever heard someone say, "I just don't know where it all goes?" If you ever catch yourself saying that, you need to change your habits. You've got to be faithful with little so you can rule over much. Unfortunately, the poor don't measure, don't pay attention, and then wonder why nothing is left over.

SEVEN HABITS OF THE POOR

#1: THE POOR SPEND MONEY UNNECESSARILY

When I was in grade 5, a bully stomped on my feet as I was changing out of my outdoor boots into my indoor shoes. This upset me so much I cried to my mom when I got home, and she phoned his mom. Then, to make me feel better, my mom fixed me a plate of my favorite foods. This developed into a bad habit, so anytime something went wrong, I'd look for a bag of chips, chocolate chip cookies, or my favorite donut.

This habit was so ingrained in me it took me years to actually recognize it and learn to control it. Now, instead of eating when I'm emotional or upset, I go for a run, a walk, or some other sort of exercise. Getting the exercise is healthier for my mind as well my body.

I developed a similar bad habit as a teenager with my finances. When I felt bad or had a bad day, I'd buy myself a pair of jeans, a new CD, or something else to soothe me. It's been proven that when you shop, the chemical dopamine is released in the brain, contributing to feelings of happiness. This can become a real disorder or addiction.

Just the other day, I felt overwhelmed because I had a lack of clarity and was juggling too much. I quickly started blaming my computer—the battery was dying too quickly, and the hard drive wasn't big enough. I knew that Apple had just released the new MacBook Air, and within 30 minutes I had convinced myself to spend $3000 on a new laptop I didn't need. I was looking for a quick fix, and I'm glad I have the awareness now to recognize when this happens. Spending money we don't have on items we don't need only leads us into debt and for completely unnecessary reasons.

I've done this with my iPhone so many times, thinking I have to have the latest one because it would help with my business… and there goes another $800 on a new phone. It's amazing how we justify certain purchases in our minds. Buying a new iPhone isn't going to bring in more business! Here's what would bring in more business: taking the time to get quiet and think about how I can help someone, in turn charging for my services.

Some people create their own storms and then get upset when it rains.

— Unknown

#2: THE POOR ARE NOT CAREFUL ABOUT WHERE THEY GET INFORMATION

Having the wrong information can hurt you and ignorance is not bliss. Years ago I was in such a rush to re-sign a record contract that I didn't hire an entertainment lawyer like I usually do. Instead I had a friend—who isn't a specialist in this field—coach me through the process. Without the specific knowledge we needed to navigate such a detailed contract, I made one big error: I neglected to negotiate on how long the label would have rights to my album. I signed a deal that was for seven years when I could have easily negotiated for five. Within those two short years, I missed out on tens of thousands of dollars in royalties because I asked the wrong person for advice.

Lack of information keeps the poor stuck. A poor person asking another poor person for financial advice is about as silly as going to the gym and asking someone overweight how to lose weight. It sounds crazy, but it happens all the time. We need to seek advice from those who are already where we want to be.

#3: THE POOR ALLOW NEGATIVE THINKING TO CLOUD THEIR POTENTIAL

Attitude is everything when it comes to being successful and wealthy. If you think you can, you can. If you think you can't, you can't. It's as simple as that. There's a famous story of two construction workers who were moving bricks while building a cathedral. When asked what they were doing, the first man replied with a growl, "I'm just laying these dang bricks." The other worker was more optimistic in his response, answering, "I'm building a beautiful cathedral."

While the negative construction worker could only see boring bricks, his co-worker saw the full vision of what he was building—and that vision gave him a sense of purpose.

Being negative and shooting down great ideas is often the mark of the unsuccessful. This is something I used to do in my early days in the studio, when we'd be working on a song and I'd start shooting down other musicians' ideas just to be heard. It came from my own insecurity in my songwriting, and from the belief that I wasn't contributing enough to the process. I thank God I caught this bad habit early on in my career and learnt to undo it. Nobody wants to work with such negativity, and if I'd continued down that path I would not be where I am—and who I am—today.

It's too easy to blame others for our problems: the government, our boss, our parents or someone who hurt us or ripped us off in some way. It's also too easy to have one bad experience and let that hold you back from pursuing a great future. Negative people love to retell the same story over and over to anyone who will listen.

If they only knew they had the power to rewrite their story today! And that they can pursue their goals themselves, rather than waiting for someone else to show up with the money and fund their dreams for them. I'm not positive or optimistic 100% of the time but if I catch my words or thoughts leaning towards the negative, I adjust quickly because I understand the consequences.

#4: THE POOR HANG AROUND POOR PEOPLE

Show me your friends, and I'll show you your future.

It's said, and I believe it's true, that whoever you hang around not only influences your personality and attitude, but your pocketbook as well. Birds of a feather flock together—and spend their money together.

I'll never forget driving home from work one day with my buddy— we were like 21 at the time. I had pulled over to a gas station and was pumping gas when we were approached by two guys in a van who said they had some speakers to sell us. I wasn't interested, but my friend got lured in by the guy's story about these supposedly high-end speakers they had for a crazy deal. My friend at least negotiated the guy down, so I decided to put my money in too. The speakers weren't a rip-off— but did I need them, or would they make me money?

No, it was a luxury, and I could have invested that money in something else, like studio time to record a song which would be an asset, making me money and impacting lives. It was a perfect example of being led and influenced by those you hang out with. Those speakers are probably in a garbage heap somewhere by now.

#5: THE POOR HAVE LITTLE PATIENCE

Patience is hard to have under many circumstances, but when it comes to buying luxuries, an added dose is required. It's easy to fall into the trap of purchasing things via payments and layaway. Credit card companies know how easy it is to get us to swipe for that vacation we feel we deserve. Many people will refinance their home to put in a pool, fix up the kitchen, or get the basement finished. Instead of waiting until they have the cash, they want it right now.

I've been subject to this myself, and had to learn the hard way. A few days before our first-year anniversary, we realized we had made it through the first year of marriage. So of course that meant we had to take another vacation with money we didn't have—and the next thing you know, we were on one of those vacation sites, buying a trip to Mexico. In Mexico, we were also almost up-sold on a second vacation, which I would've bought if it wasn't for Melanie talking some sense into me!

It's very easy to be lured into purchasing things we don't need or have the money for right now because we're addicted to that dopamine hit. I'm trained in sales, and I know that tactics like fear of missing out (FOMO) or limited quantities or time can push someone into a purchase. If you do have a great product and you're trying to sell something that's helpful, that's fine. I'm talking about recognizing the methods that trick people into buying things they can't afford and should wait and save up for. My advice, if you're about to make a big purchase, is to sleep on it. Wait a few days to decide if you really need it, or if you're giving in to a spur-of-the-moment impulse.

#6: THE POOR TRADE TIME FOR MONEY

One of the biggest revelations I've had in the last few years was to stop trading my time for money. One of the main reasons the poor are poor—and I'm also talking about hard-working middle-class families here—is because they only get paid when they're at their job. When I was at my IT job, even though it was a salaried position, if I stopped working, I would stop getting paid. If you work at Starbucks, you only get paid when you're standing there making drinks. If you don't punch that clock, you don't get paid, so your income is based on your ability to work. What if you get sick or get in an accident? Sure, you might get a few days of sick pay, but then what?

Rich people invest their time building an asset: creating something for a period of time while not getting paid. Then, because they invested their time, that asset then pays them for a lifetime. A perfect example would be this book. I wrote it and recorded it once. Now it's online, available for the whole world to purchase forever. I can even pass it down to my children if I want.

You want to be able to make money without having to trade your time. What I love about my business is that even if I decide to go on a vacation or take a day to skateboard with my daughter, money still comes in. You spend money every day, so you should create money every day. This is where multiple streams of income come in: you earn money without it requiring your presence. In the next chapter, I'm going to help you brainstorm a bunch of ideas in which you invest your time once and get paid forever.

#7: THE POOR FOCUS ON THE MINOR INSTEAD OF THE MAJOR

Have you ever heard your parents or spouse say, "You left the light on again," or "Close the door, I'm not trying to heat the garden"? What about running the laundry and dishwasher at night to try and save a couple bucks? My favorite is driving 30 minutes completely out of the way to save a little by getting cheaper gas or groceries. These are all noble ideas at the beginning of your journey to financial freedom, but there comes a time where you've got to dream bigger.

Your time is a thousand times more valuable than trying to save a few bucks here and there. I've never heard of anyone becoming a millionaire from turning off all the lights or not leaving the water running while they brush their teeth (though both are good for the environment). We call this focusing on the minor things in life while missing the major. You want to be dreaming up income-earning ideas so you don't have to worry about whether you left the light on or when to run the dishwasher. Focus on that big idea that will bring in thousands instead of worrying about a few dollars.

It's not about what you earn, it's what you do with what you earn.

— Jim Rohn

WHICH HABITS DO YOU CHOOSE?

Take some time to look at the habits of the poor and the rich, and see which habits you need to break and which habits you need to start to develop. In my book, Fighter, I talk about sowing a thought, because once you sow a thought, you reap an action, and once you sow an action, you reap a habit, and once you sow a habit, you reap your character, and when you sow your character, you reap a destiny. I'm talking about your financial destiny for you and your family. Don't despise small beginnings. By implementing good financial habits into your life and removing bad ones, you can start your journey to financial liberty.

" FORMAL EDUCATION
WILL MAKE YOU
A LIVING;
SELF-EDUCATION
WILL MAKE YOU
A FORTUNE."

— JIM ROHN

CHAPTER 4

MILLION-DOLLAR LIFE LESSONS I LEARNED FROM PLAYING MONOPOLY WITH MY FOUR-YEAR-OLD

A good man leaves an inheritance to his children's children,

But the wealth of the sinner is stored up for the righteous.

— Proverbs 13:22

When playing the game Monopoly, everyone knows you have to roll the dice to move forward. You have to purchase and invest in the properties you land on in order to get wealthy, charge rent, and win the game. Yet in the game of life, many of us are scared to roll the dice on our dreams, and most people just move around the board, barely passing "Go" by collecting a paycheck that doesn't provide financial freedom. Life is a game, and so many of us jump into it without reading the rules first.

When my daughter turned four years old, all of a sudden the Monopoly board started coming out, and we played it every night. She loved it. As I taught her about money and how to buy and sell properties, I realized some incredible lessons were right under my nose—lessons no one had taught me.

If you've never played Monopoly, the goal is to go around the board and purchase three properties of the same color so you can build houses and then hotels on them. When other players land on them, they have to pay higher rent. Whoever has the most properties and money wins.

As a kid, I loved playing Monopoly. I can remember Friday nights with different friends and family around the dinner table, with chips, pop, and cookies, playing into the night. I always wanted to buy Boardwalk and Park Place because they were the most valuable properties. The lessons that can be learned from this game and applied to real life are simple but profound, and they can change your life.

GET IN THE GAME

Nobody has a monopoly on good ideas.
– Kevin O'Leary

If you want to win at anything, you have to play the game. So many of us just sit on the sidelines, watching others play while we only dream of doing what they do. Some of us even criticize those around us to make ourselves feel better about our lack of action. I say roll the freaking dice and get in the game!

Out of the 40 spaces on the Monopoly board, there are three spaces called "Chance," which require you to pick up and obey a Chance card. Sometimes you pick it up and you've inherited $100; other times you're instructed to pay each player $50. Life is filled with chances, and if you want any type of financial success, you have to take some risks. My hero, Peter J. Daniels, says, "The more you insulate yourself from risk, the more you insulate yourself from success."

THE RISKS I TOOK

I'm writing this part of the book during the COVID-19 crisis, and it's extremely sad to see people lose their jobs. This is the thing about working for others: you have no control over whether or not you keep your job and your livelihood. Your employment situation is dependent on your boss or whoever owns the company—the one who took the risk in starting a business in the first place. I like to think that going into business is a lot less risky than being at the whim of an employer who could fire you with little or no notice.

One way to minimize risk is to be as informed as possible about any investment or venture you want to get involved in. As I mentioned in Chapter One, I took a huge risk in quitting my job to pursue my music career. Everyone thought I was crazy because I left a great-paying job to follow my dream, and the risks were very real: we could have lost our home if I hadn't been able to pay the mortgage.

We went $30,000 in debt pretty quickly, but this experience taught me how to become an entrepreneur and how to work for myself. Most importantly, it taught me to create my way out of debt by looking for opportunities to make money.

If I hadn't taken that risk, I never would have had the life experiences I've had, traveling to 22 countries to sing about Jesus. So I say, take a chance—but do it wisely! If I could go back and do it over, I would have quit my job a little slower. I still would have done it, but I'd have taken the time to make a clear budget and a better plan.

Melanie and I took another chance when we decided to rent our condo and buy another property, rather than just selling the condo we currently lived in. Of course we heard all the horror stories about bad tenants, but our tenant contacted us maybe once a year, if that, and normally it was because he wanted me to pick up the next years' post-dated checks. (I know checks are a little old-school, but we hadn't set up direct deposit yet.)

This was my first attempt at passive income, and it was awesome. Passive income is money generated in the background while you're working on something else. Sometimes it requires some minimal work and upkeep, but not much. Our tenant was paying off my mortgage for me! We rented that place out for three years without any disruption.

Four years later, we were in our new home and loving it when we felt God calling us to move to California. So again, instead of selling our home, we decided to rent it out, but this time we hired a property management company to take care of finding a tenant. The first tenant was a doctor. He had good money coming in, but he failed to reveal that he had six kids.

While they were a disaster in some ways (they threw constant parties, damaged the hardwood floor, and we had to get all three toilets replaced) luckily, they ended up leaving pretty quickly. After they'd left, another family moved in for three years without a problem. So yes, we took risks, and there were some challenges, but we just dealt with them as they came. Take chances and get in the game!

Don't allow a lack of money to determine how big you dream.

— Manafest

INCOME TAX

Back to the Monopoly board, and just four spaces up from Go, there's a space called "Income Tax." When you land on it, you have to pay 10% of all you own, or $200. As a kid I always hated landing on that spot, but I never understood what income tax was! Nobody ever told me, and it frustrates me just thinking about it, because income tax is one of the largest expenses you pay almost all your life, depending on the country you live in.

I only learned about income tax a full year after working in my first job (the one at the computer company for $13.50 an hour). After a whole year of making what I thought was a lot of money, driving my own car, living at home, and taking my then-girlfriend out to fancy McDonald's dinners, tax time came around. "What?" I said to my mom. "Why the heck do I have to file taxes, and how do you even do that?"

I cannot freaking believe I went to school for all those years and no one, no one... I'm so ticked off right now... NO ONE taught me about income tax or how to file my taxes or save money on taxes.

I had a friend file my taxes, and all I can say is I got smashed in the face with a huge tax bill of about $4,000. And as a 20 year old, I was freaking out. I ended up writing the government 12 post-dated checks until it was paid off.

As the Bible says clearly, "People perish for a lack of knowledge." Good, nice, evil, kind—doesn't matter, you will perish if you don't have the right information. In my case, it was a lack of financial education. Thanks, teachers, for teaching me nothing about money.

So how could this have been avoided? With tax write-offs. If you own a home-based business, you can write off a lot of your expenses. I could have written off my car expenses, gas, some food, and if I paid rent at home, rent. Of course, see a certified tax accountant for proper legal advice, but a good accountant can save you tens of thousands of dollars. Because I'm in the music business, I hire an accountant who specializes in my type of business. Taxes are your biggest expense, so it makes sense to learn how to minimize them as much as possible.

Unfortunately, if you work a job, there isn't a ton you can do, but if you go into business—which is what I'm going to encourage you to do—then there are ways you can reduce your taxes.

The point to remember is that what the government gives,

it must first take away.

— John S. Coleman

INVEST IN PROPERTY

When I was a kid playing Monopoly, if I landed on a property like New York Avenue, I'd be asked, "Do you want to buy it?" But when I started playing with my daughter, I thought to myself, no I don't want to buy that property, I want to invest in that property.

There's a big difference between buying something and investing in it. When you invest in something, your goal is that it will pay you income back later. For instance, if I buy a property for $100 and someone lands on it, they have to pay me $10 rent, and I just made back 10% of my purchase. I only need to have someone land on it nine more times and I've made all of my money back, plus I still own the property. Pretty awesome deal.

Buy land. They're not making it anymore.

— Mark Twain

Here's a real-world example. Say you buy a foreclosed house for a huge discount: $140,000. You invest some time and money: you clean it up, fix it, renovate it. Now you can sell it for $200,000 or rent it out for much more than you could have done before you renovated it.

We did this for a property in Tennessee; instead of selling, we decided to rent it, because we wanted the monthly cash flow. In this case, cash flow is the rent someone pays you (minus the property taxes, mortgage, maintenance and insurance payments).

If the rental income is $1500, the property taxes are $300, and your mortgage is $300, you're netting $900 positive cash flow every month. Someone else is paying your mortgage for you, and hopefully the house is also appreciating in value. This is why it's important to look at a lot of houses to understand the market before buying the first place you see.

I've heard many different real estate professionals recommend that you look at between 10 and 100 houses to get a good gauge of the market. How do you really know you're getting a good deal if you have nothing to compare it to?

If you can find a motivated seller who needs to sell quick because they're re-locating for a job or other unforeseen circumstances, you can get a house at under market value. There's a perspective shift required here: you don't make money when you sell but when you buy a property. And every dollar you save in the deal adds up because there are always closing costs, legal fees, land transfer tax and other administration costs to account for.

I'll go deeper into investing in cash-flowing properties later in this book. Ninety percent of all millionaires become so through owning real estate. More money has been made in real estate than in all industry combined.

The wise young man or wage earner of today invests his money in real estate.

— Andrew Carnegie

SAVE FOR A RAINY DAY

Some people play Monopoly like they'll never run out of money. They buy every property they land on until they have no cash left. Then they land on my property and have to mortgage one of their properties just to pay me $16 rent. Some people do the same thing in the real world. As soon as they get money, they spend it. They don't save it, and they definitely don't invest it.

If you cannot save, then the seeds of success are not in you.

— Peter J. Daniels

I can't stress enough how important it is to have financial reserves. Sometimes the car needs to be repaired. The air conditioner or dishwasher breaks, or you get that speeding ticket on the way to work. Living paycheck to paycheck is stressful. Not only does having financial reserves protect you during a storm, but when a great deal comes around, you can take advantage of an opportunity if you have some money saved up.

Plan your future, because you have to live in it.

— Robert Schuller

BUY ASSETS INSTEAD OF LUXURIES

Between my favorite two properties on the Monopoly board, Boardwalk and Park Place, there is a space called "Luxury" with a giant diamond ring on it. As a kid playing the game, I didn't even know what luxury meant; I just knew I didn't want to buy a diamond ring, because

I'd rather buy another property or house so I could win the game.

Everyone knows that to win the game of Monopoly, you need assets and not luxuries, yet in the real world, what does the majority of the population do? They invest in luxuries instead of property. It's pretty hard to get wealthy when you spend all your money on things like new cars, big screen TVs, eating out, video games, and jewelry. The rich get rich while investing in assets that make them money, like cash-flowing rental properties.

I visit people who say they can't afford to invest, yet they have the most expensive flat screen TV, a fancy car, and the latest smartphone. I'm not against having these things, but they don't put money in your pocket, they take money out of your pocket.

USE ASSETS TO GENERATE PASSIVE INCOME

If you want to win the game of life, you need to start investing in assets like real estate and other passive income-generating opportunities. Nothing is ever 100% passive, but these projects definitely don't require eight hours a day to manage.

For instance, I write songs. Some of the songs I wrote 10 years ago still earn me an income today. The same is true with books: years after you write a book, people continue to buy it or download the digital version, and you get paid royalties. Now, I can hear you doubting. "I can't write a book!" Why not? I'm sure there's something you are super passionate about and could give others guidance on.

It only takes 10 minutes on Google to type in "How to…" to come up with a bunch of ideas. What if someone searched for "How to change oil on a Mercedes," and your book or online course popped up? I got a flat tire recently, and had never changed a tire in my life. I called my wife and all of my friends, and no one was able to help me. I did a quick search on YouTube and there was this guy teaching me step by step how to change a flat tire.

What's really interesting is that an ad played before his video. This is because the guy who made the video and owns the YouTube channel is monetizing his channel with ads—so he got paid a small royalty for that video he filmed years ago. Six years ago I created a tutorial video on how to upload your music online so I could help other musicians get their music out there. I had no idea some simple little video that was common knowledge to me would get tens of thousands of views and earn me royalties on YouTube.

I'll share more passive income ideas later on, but I want to at least plant the seed in your mind that there are business ideas sitting right under your nose that can generate income. It's more than possible. I get excited about this because I know the freedom it can provide for you and your family.

TIME AND SPEED MATTER: ROLL DOUBLES

You should've seen my daughter's face the first time she rolled doubles and I told her she got to go again. Sometimes she'd roll doubles twice in a row, opening up two opportunities for her to win the game. She was delighted!

First, she had two opportunities to buy properties before me and make money right away if I landed on them. In the real world, if someone gets the deal before you do, you miss out.

We bought a new home recently because I saw a for-sale sign that said, "Coming soon." I called the realtor and asked him if we could see the place. We were the first ones to see it, and when we put in an offer, it was accepted. He told me a lot of people were ticked off because they didn't get a shot at putting in an offer—at which point they might have bid the price up. So, he who strikes first has the best chance of winning.

And second, in Monopoly, the quicker you get around the board, the faster you pass GO and collect $200.

Good timing is also a key part of selling, especially when it comes to your house or other personal assets. I had two friends who wanted to sell their house during a hot market, when people were paying way over the asking price and bidding wars were common. One friend put his house up for sale right near the end of this boom. He still got a good price, but not as much as if he had listed it just two weeks prior. Another friend waited even longer, and his house was on the market for months; he had to lower the price significantly before it finally sold.

This leads me to one more lesson involving time: procrastination. Sometimes people playing Monopoly keep rolling the dice and landing on properties, but they don't buy because they're waiting for that one specific deal. I'm guilty of this occasionally—when I've got my eye on one of the more expensive properties and I want to make sure I have the money ready when I land on it. But the key—and we're talking real life now—is to not procrastinate to the extent that you pass up on tons of opportunities right in front of you.

Let me tell you something: there is never going to be a perfect time or a perfect deal. You just have to get started. If you're afraid you're gonna make a mistake, let me be the first to tell you that you will. You'll make lots of them, but you'll learn powerful lessons. A boxer knows when they get in the ring they are going to get hit. It's inevitable. Life is going to hit you with failures and mistakes, but you, too, need to learn how to get up and hit back.

Successful people make decisions quickly (as soon as all the facts are available) and change them very slowly (if ever).

Successful people make decisions quickly (as soon as all the facts are available) and change them very slowly (if ever). Unsuccessful people make decisions very slowly, and change them often and quickly.

– Napoleon Hill

UTILITIES, SUBSCRIPTIONS, AND GETTING PAID OVER AND OVER AGAIN

As a kid playing Monopoly, I never liked to buy the utilities Water Works or Electric Company, because you couldn't buy houses or put hotels on them. The max you could make was $120 (when someone rolled 12 and had to pay ten times the amount shown on the dice). But in real life, if you own a utility company or invest in a technology like that, the potential for income is exponentially higher.

Think about it. You pay the electric company and water company every month. They've got you and I as customers for life! We call this a subscription business, or a recurring income model. The TV, cable, and internet companies, as well as Netflix, are doing the exact same thing. These businesses are built on subscriptions, and they scale it to the thousands and millions of customers. It's extremely powerful because it's a lot easier to keep a customer than to get a new one.

Better to do something imperfectly than nothing flawlessly.
— Robert Schuller

Even health companies have subscription programs where they deliver fresh fruits and vegetables to people's houses for a monthly fee. I saw a subscription for dogs, where you get a dog box delivered each month with new toys and other products.

In the music business, we have fan clubs or Patreon pages; if you go way back, there was a company called Columbia House, where you could join the CD of the Month Club. (I just dated myself with that.) Governments are the best at it, though, because they have you paying property taxes every single month to keep that money coming in, and if they don't get you there, they take it out of your paycheck every week (or quarterly if you own the business).

The subscription model also works for service-based companies like dentists who get you to come in for your bi-annual teeth cleaning, or chiropractors who sign you up for your weekly adjustments. There is big money in the recurring revenue model when it comes to business.

Now, instead of getting frustrated, ask the question, "How can I benefit from this?" I've seen people create a T-shirt subscription club for a specific niche where subscribers get the latest shirt every month. I'm personally part of a soap subscription for a healthy men's soap called Dr. Squatch.

The possibilities are endless, but the aim is the same: to build a recurring income stream. It's much better than a customer buying once and then leaving. You want customers coming back again automatically, building stability and predictability into your business.

I HEARD JAY ABRAHAM SAY THERE ARE THREE WAYS TO GROW A BUSINESS:

1. Increase the number of customers
2. Increase the average transaction value (raise your prices or add upsells)
3. Increase the frequency of repurchase: get recurring value out of each customer

GO DIRECTLY TO JAIL: HANGING WITH THE WRONG CROWD

"Go directly to jail, do not pass GO, do not collect $200 dollars." In a game of Monopoly, this is frustrating but funny, because you know you'll get out of jail in a couple of turns and be back in the game. But when you mess around and break the law in real life, the penalties are more serious.

Illegal business transactions, driving when drunk, cheating on your taxes, or sleeping around on your spouse could be the downfall of your whole business as well as your character. How many people have lost it all because they got seduced by opportunity and the love of money? I don't have a problem with getting things, as long as those things don't get you.

There's no right way to do the wrong thing.

— Peter J. Daniels

In the movie South Paw, Jake Gyllenhaal plays the character Billy Hope. Billy has money, success, and a beautiful, supportive wife and daughter. But because of his temper and who he hangs around with, he flies off the handle at a press event and his wife gets killed. He continues on a rampage, losing his car and house, and has to start all over again.

As I tour the world with different artists and meet different people, I see two types of success. There is a light side, where people do business with nothing hiding in the closet. But there's also a dark side, where I can just tell there are drugs and other sketchy behaviors going on that I just don't want to be a part of.

You can go into business, make a ton of money, give back, and make a difference—all while avoiding the dark side that tends to seduce.

Now is the time to stop drifting and wake up—to assess yourself, the people around you, and the direction in which you are headed in as cold and brutal a light as possible. Without fear.

— 50 Cent

PAYING THE PRICE OF DIVORCE

The older I get, sadly the more divorces I witness among friends and family. I read in Stefan Aarnio's book Hard Times Create Strong Men, "Divorce doesn't just take 50% of your wealth. Divorce usually destroys 70% of your wealth and also your mental, physical, emotional, and spiritual self."

I haven't experienced divorce but I know first-hand how difficult it is to concentrate or get any work done after I've just had a fight with my wife. My heart is pounding and I feel like my energy is zapped until I make things right.

As Stefan says, "A divorce can rob you of all your momentum in life, your purpose, your business, your company, your children, your family and drag out for 5, 10 or even 20 years after the marriage separates."

There are, of course, situations where staying in a marriage is unhealthy or even dangerous, and if that's the case I sincerely hope you choose to get outside guidance to help to deal with your circumstances. But there are also times when we've simply lost a little of the spark that brought us together, or we foolishly think the grass is greener elsewhere.

In those cases, before leaving your current spouse or contemplating an affair I suggest you think long and hard of the devastation and havoc you will wreak in your life, business and family. Stupid games win stupid prizes.

WINNING THE GAME

I continue to teach my daughter math and the basic principles of investing as we play Monopoly, but the game isn't over yet. The game of life you are playing right now is not over yet, either, and if you're reading this, you're still in it. The question is, how can you change your investing strategy so you and your family can win this game?

"BETTER TO DO SOMETHING IMPERFECTLY THAN NOTHING FLAWLESSLY."

— ROBERT SCHULLER

CHAPTER 5

WHY I LOVE SWISS CURRENCY BEST

SWISS stands for "Sales While I Sleep Soundly."

— Manafest

I can't think of a better currency to be paid in than one that flows in while I'm sleeping. The idea of making money while you sleep might sound too good to be true, but it's real. The good news is, the opportunity to earn SWISS dollars isn't only for the super-rich, but everyday people like you and me.

And please hold off any skepticism. Open your mind during this chapter. I used to be very suspicious of get-rich-quick schemes, but what's worse: a get-rich-quick scheme or a stay-broke-the-rest-of-your-life scheme? As I recently learned from a talk from my friend Myron Golden, scheme comes from the word schematic, which means having a set of plans. I think we can all agree that one of the reasons we aren't more wealthy or successful is because we lack a plan to follow. Instead, we just follow the crowd.

My first taste of SWISS came after I had written a few songs back in 2001. A friend told me I had to register them with a company called SOCAN so I'd get paid royalties.

At the time, I was only writing songs because I wanted to perform them on stage, rocking out with people and telling them about Jesus. I wasn't thinking my songs would ever make me money—especially not while I was sleeping. But because I own the publishing rights to those songs and they are monetized correctly, to this day I still get paid for songs I wrote almost two decades ago.

With the advent of internet technology, thousands of people 24/7 across the world listen to my music via Spotify, Apple Music, and YouTube, earning me royalties while I sleep. The concept of creating something once and having it continue to earn money for many years was once a foreign concept to me—but once I got it, I was hooked. Making SWISS isn't unique to the music industry. It works for real estate, inventions, info products, online businesses, and many other examples I'll share later in this book.

The most common way to earn money—the opposite of SWISS— is trading your time for dollars. We are all familiar with working for a company in exchange for a paycheck. This could be a paper route, working at Starbucks, managing people at an office, or working in construction. Even if you work for yourself as a consultant and people pay you a high fee, you're still trading your time for dollars. The problem I have with this scenario is when you stop working, the paychecks stop too.

When I stop working, I still get paid, because of all the SWISS systems I've built over the years. Imagine working at building something and not getting paid right away. That's a little hard to take, but once you've put in the work and it's built, you now have a system that pays you forever. Pretty awesome, right?

You can compare SWISS dollars to catching a wave on a surfboard. You have to do the work up-front by paddling out there and getting smacked in the face with waves. But once you're out past the break, the water is smooth. Now all you have to do is wait for the right wave, start paddling in, and cruise with the waves' momentum. That momentum is what we're building in a SWISS system.

TAKING A RISK FOR FREEDOM

What we're really talking about here is freedom.

• Freedom to take a whole month off work to travel.

• Freedom to coach your kid's soccer game with no stress.

• Freedom to help out with family or your local church or charity.

• Freedom to pursue that passion project or write that book.

I want to challenge you to be willing to take the risk up front so you can reap the rewards in the future. Everything in life is risky. Can you show me a self-made millionaire who didn't take any risks? They don't exist. Just like when you risk being heartbroken by opening your heart to someone you love, I'm asking you to open your mind and your wallet to take a risk for your financial freedom.

As I was about to turn 40, I thought to myself, I wish I'd taken even more risks when I was younger, because I'd be even more successful. For a brief moment, I wondered if it was too late, like I'd missed the boat. But then I realized my 60-year-old and 70-year-old selves will be saying the same thing, so take some risks now! My friend Pastor Brendan Witton said, "Life is more than going to school to get a degree to get a job to get a house and a spouse and 2.5 kids so you can retire and then die." If I'm a slave to a J.O.B (which stands for "Just Over Broke"), I don't have flexibility. I remember what it was like to wake up every morning at 6:00 a.m. to drive to work for an hour to work on someone else's dream every day.

Now I wake up at 6:00 a.m. to work on my own dreams, if I choose. When I take my daughter to school I see a lot of other parents dropping off their kids, but Melanie and I are the only couple there at the same time. I get the pleasure of surprising my daughter every day, and that's why I'm so passionate about this—because I want to open your eyes to building a business that pays you SWISS dollars while giving you a lifestyle of freedom.

If you don't build your dream, someone will hire you to help build theirs.

– Tony Gaskins

WHAT'S MORE VALUABLE: TIME OR MONEY?

As I've already stated, you can always make more money, but you cannot make any more time. At the end of our lives, we are all going to have more money than time left over. My suggestion is to invest your money to buy back as much time as possible. The first thing you have to do is put a dollar value on your time. How much is your time worth?

If I can write a song, create a product, or provide a service valued up to $1000 an hour, then I probably shouldn't be doing jobs that I can pay someone else $8 an hour to do, such as ship out an order, wash my car, or handle customer service.

As a human, you have 24 hours in a day, but as an entrepreneur, you have 24 hours, PLUS the time of anyone who works for you and is on your team.

— *Caleb Maddix*

I received an email from Joe Polish of the Genius Network that included a very cool conversation he had with Richard Branson. Joe asked Richard, "When's the last time you went to a grocery store?" Richard looked at Joe and said, "I don't think I've ever been to a grocery store." Joe said, "What do you mean? How is it possible you've never gone to a grocery store?" Then he asked Richard, "Well, when's the last time you did laundry?" And Richard said, "I've never done laundry." Perplexed, Joe said, "What do you mean, you've never done laundry? What about when you were a kid?" "My mum did my laundry," Richard said. Then Richard simply said, "Joe, you hire people to do that stuff. Taking the time to hire the right person will save you thousands of hours in your life."

Are you starting to get the picture? This idea helped me focus on my highest-value labor and stop spending my time on lower-level tasks I can delegate to someone else.

A lot of people struggle because they've never put a dollar value on what their time is worth. Even some small business owners never put together a price list for their services, they just make it up when people ask. If you haven't done this yet, stop reading this book and put a dollar figure to your time. If you don't know what to charge, see what your competitors are charging. Then make sure you provide more value than they do, and charge more.

It is so easy to sell ourselves short because we don't believe our own worth. The best advice I ever got was "Raise your prices." Another great nugget was "Stop trading your life for a pittance at a job and start getting paid what you're worth."

When you learn how much you're worth, you'll stop giving people discounts.
— Karen Salmansohn

CREATE YOUR OWN SWISS DOLLAR PLAN

Here's one of the differences between the rich and the poor (and I'm not just talking about poor in regard to money, but in regard to time as well): when you work for someone else, you are spending your time. When you work for yourself to create something, you are investing your time. We've all witnessed very successful businesspersons who have lots of money, but no time to spend with family or enjoy life. What if you started creating products today that you could sell over and over again? You'd be leveraging yourself: you do the work once, but continue to get paid for it for potentially years to come.

Be careful creating a service-based business, especially if you are doing the service, because generally, the more successful you are, the busier you become, and the less time you have.

Stress and pressure need to be factored in as well. I remember what it was like being asked to perform every weekend: I was run ragged flying all over the world and not getting much sleep. This is a common problem in industries where people provide a service. Think about hair stylists, chefs, painters, carpenters, dentists—their service is reliant on their presence. Sure, they can keep raising their prices, which makes more money—but if they want to serve more people—or have more time for themselves—they'll have to hire someone to work with them, or for them.

I have some friends who are really good at mixing songs, producing music, creating art, and fixing computers. The only way they can free up their time is to delegate a project to a contractor or perhaps a virtual assistant, but some customers want them working on the project, not a random person they don't know.

I have the same problem when performing as Manafest. I could play hundreds of dates in a year, and at one time I was—but I never saw my wife. That's why I made the lifestyle change to not perform as much. I can only physically be in one place at one time, but by utilizing technology and the internet, I can broadcast the show live for thousands of people at once. One way we are thinking of leveraging my performing is to stream a show and sell online tickets so the world can watch.

Melanie has started to rethink her business in a similar way. She was constantly getting hired to do graphic design for clients—whether it was creating brochures, logos, album artwork, magazines—you name it, she would design it. Then one night we went for a walk and got an idea. Instead of designing for all these different clients, why shouldn't she design for herself? Why not create art prints with inspirational messages on them and sell them? This is when her company, Vision City Art Studio, was birthed, and she was soon shipping art all over the world.

It's funny because over the years, usually at my most exhausted, I'd wonder how I could clone myself so I could get my message and my music out there without me being there. I'd wonder how I could keep this machine running while I was sleeping, or on vacation, or playing with my daughter. I remember Kenneth Copeland saying he wanted to get the message of Jesus preached around the world on every available device. Now he owns the network "Victory" that preaches the good news 24/7 around the world nonstop. How can you do something similar in your business? How can you take yourself out of it?

Time is free, but it's priceless.
You can't own it, but you can use it.
You can't keep it, but you can spend it.
Once you've lost it, you can never get it back.
— Harvey Mackay

10 WAYS YOU CAN START EARNING SWISS

1. SONGWRITING

I write a song once and it earns royalties forever. My most popular song, which generates the majority of my income, was written over 12 years ago. This is common for artists all over the world, and it's why they make "Greatest Hits" albums. However this takes a lot of upfront work and an investment of time, money and patience. Unless you feel 100% called to this, don't expect to turn a profit overnight.

Ideas become powerful only when acted upon—so do it now.

— Manafest

2. WRITING A BOOK

You could write a book that helps people, and every time the book is sold, you get paid. I'm sure you have a story or an experience that others would love to read about. I wrote my first book the best I could, and then hired a co-writer to finish it off. It doesn't have to be a literary work of art; it just has to help someone. It could be fiction, for children, self-help, or a "how to" book. If you really hate writing, pick up your phone, dictate it, and sell it as an audiobook on audible. com. That is one of my favorite ways to consume books, and I know I'm not alone, because millions of people drive or ride to work each day listening to books. Don't think you need a book publisher either, Amazon's self publishing tool KDP has made it very accessible for anyone to self-publish their own book and at no cost.

3. SELL YOUR ART

As I mentioned, my wife began her journey into SWISS dollars when she started creating art products. She created art prints with messages on them that said, "I love you," "Never give up," or "Coffee first." At first, she was shipping these out herself, which required a lot of time when she'd get dozens of orders. She took SWISS dollars a step further when she digitized her art prints—now people can download and print them out themselves. This requires no time at all for Melanie and it happens automatically. All Melanie has to do is size the images and make them available. You can visit her website for more info at https://visioncity.biz.

4. JEWELRY AND APPAREL

I have friends who sell jewelry and apparel like necklaces, bracelets, T-shirts, and hats. Some of these items are custom-made, which requires a lot of time, and attention to detail. The products are spectacular but if you get too many orders, it's hard to sustain any sort of massive growth. One of my friends found a great manufacturer and pressed large quantities of shirts, keeping the same quality. His products are now shipped to customers all over the world, so he can focus on the business instead of being in the trenches. Remember, we want to take you out of the business so you can focus on growing the business. This doesn't mean you can't be creative; in fact, it frees you up to create more.

5. AGRICULTURE

I met a woman at a seminar who owns a cocoa bean farm. I know another guy who owns a blueberry farm. I've heard of real estate deals where you (the investor) buy the land and the farmer rents it from you, providing you with both income from the real estate and the crops. People will always need food and shelter and now more than ever they are willing to pay a premium for healthy organic food. This is a demand that is only going to increase as health becomes a bigger priority for people.

6. OWN A BUSINESS OR FRANCHISE

If you bought a Starbucks franchise and hired the right team and manager, you'd only have to put in a certain number of hours a month. This would take a larger upfront investment, but if you're passionate about coffee, you're buying into a system that already works. You might have ambitions to open your own coffee shop in the future— and this is a great way to get experience and come to understand all the ins and outs of the industry first, giving you a much higher chance of future success.

7. ONLINE COURSES

I love the fact that technology has taken us to the place where you can share your knowledge by turning it into an online course that you then sell. If you're not sure what you could create a course in, open up Google or YouTube and type "How to." Google will tell you what the most popular searches are: in other words, what kind of help people look for the most. For instance, the phrase "lose weight on keto" is currently searched on YouTube 22,100 times a month.

What if you created a course that helps people with that? There's a good chance that people would buy a course, get coaching, or read a book on that topic. The online course industry is currently a multi-billion-dollar industry, and will only continue to grow. Don't assume that everyone else knows what you know—often they don't, and they're actually willing to pay to learn from you. (More information on online courses is coming in Chapter Seven.)

8. AFFILIATE MARKETING

Affiliate marketing is a commission-based business where you are paid by a company for recommending other peoples' products. What's great about this is you don't have any inventory or upfront costs and you can get started for free. For instance, if you sign up with Amazon's associate affiliate program, they give you a special username and password so you can create affiliate links for the millions of products they have in their store. If you love this book, you can grab an affiliate link from Amazon, and if people buy this book based on your recommendation, Amazon will pay you a commission.

What's even cooler is, if they buy anything else after they click on your link, you get commission on the full order! Writing one recommendation might get you multiple commissions. I make thousands of dollars a year recommending products, software, and books to friends and fans. Some people write book reviews or make 'open box' videos for certain products, then they put their affiliate link to that product below the video or blog post.

9. SUBSCRIPTIONS

Just like the utility company model we talked about in the previous chapter, it's easier to keep customers than find new ones. With a subscription service, instead of that customer paying you once and leaving, they sign up and pay you month after month. I have a coaching program for musicians to help them market and monetize their music called Fanbase University.

Twice a month, I go live online via video and answer questions for an hour. People pay a monthly fee, and I show up once or twice a month, coaching hundreds at a time. Consider what you can offer using this model: T-shirts, handmade chocolates, homemade soap, expert advice, chapters of a novel you're writing… the possibilities are endless. A good place to start is to think of something that people need to re-fill like supplements, cosmetics, and other products that get used up.

10. REAL ESTATE

As we've covered, a very popular avenue to create financial freedom is owning and renting real estate. Real estate has made more millionaires than almost any other investment out there. Not only are you provided with a monthly income, but in most cases, it appreciates in value. I don't know any other physical asset that you can buy with only 20-25% down but get 100% of the appreciation of the total value of the property. That is SWISS dollar leverage strategy to the max. Imagine getting monthly checks from your renters: instead of the first of the month being bill day, it's also payday!

CLOSE-UP ON REAL ESTATE

Owning real estate by purchasing a house or condo and renting it out to people every month is one of the oldest forms of SWISS dollars. It may be the most popular, so I want to give you a little more information about it, especially as I have direct experience in this area. A common way to get started in some states is to buy a duplex, live in one side of the house, and rent the other side; or you could rent out a basement apartment.

My friend Brandon at Bigger Pockets coined a "BRR strategy." This is to Buy a place, Refurbish it, and Rent it out. For example, you might see the potential in a foreclosed house, get it for a great deal, refurbish it and rent it out. Often, a run-down looking house only needs a coat of paint and maybe a new carpet or laminate flooring.

This is where having vision comes in to play again, because where one person sees a dirty house, an investor sees a great opportunity.

Another option is to buy a place, fix it up over time, live in it for a while, and then rent it out. Now, I'm not talking about flipping houses. The goal is to have multiple properties paying you SWISS dollars every month, so you have monthly cash flow coming in.

When we did this with our condo, I had to regularly pinch myself that there were real people sleeping there who paid us money every month. By the way, I definitely recommend hiring a property manager to field those middle-of-the-night calls from your tenants; sure, there's a little fee, but the peace of mind is worth its weight in gold. Having a manager frees me up so I can focus on bigger dreams. That's SWISS dollar freedom.

You become financially free when your passive income exceeds your expenses.

– T. Harv Eker

Here's a quick story that really inspired me to think big in terms of real estate. My friend Tony told me about a billionaire who purchased a commercial piece of real estate with a sports dome coliseum on it. Every month, an extra $40,000 in income appeared in this guy's account, and he had no idea where it was coming from. It wasn't until his accountant dug a little deeper that they discovered there were huge billboards on the land that were being rented out as advertising.

Imagine owning a piece of real estate that has multiple streams of income, not just from the property, but from billboards as well. I read on capitoloutdoor.com that the revenue generated from billboard companies may reach up to 40 to 50 percent before counting depreciation, taxes, amortization and interest. Not surprisingly, this billionaire focused his attention to owning land with billboards all across the USA and Canada.

HAVING THE SWISS DOLLAR MULTIPLYING MINDSET

There are dozens, if not hundreds, of other SWISS dollar adventures you can set up, but I hope those 10 ideas get you stirred up and thinking.

To make SWISS dollars work for you, you need to change your mindset. Stop thinking in terms of one customer at a time, or one-on-one. I want you to stretch your thinking to how you can shift from one-on-one to one-to-many. I hope you let that sink in, because that is a million-dollar concept. By creating a product or service that provides value to people without your presence is extremely powerful, because you are leveraging your most powerful asset, which is time.

Here are a few other things to think about in the area of SWISS dollars:

• Instead of purchasing one rental house and helping one person at a time, you can buy multi-family apartments and help many people. Our income is often determined by how many people we are helping.

• Instead of going door-to-door selling a service, you could place a radio spot or run a Facebook and Instagram ad selling the product or service automatically. When I started advertising my music online, I opened up the door to millions of customers all around the globe.

• If you're a performer, why not create a video and post it online, where it has the potential to reach an unlimited amount of people? Or perform live and broadcast via social media to people all over the world. You can even record a show to share later on YouTube, Instagram, and Facebook, impacting even more people. Monetize this via the ads that are placed around the video, or look into a platform like Patreon where fans pay a subscription to see your material exclusively.

Not only do these methods get your message, product, or service out to more people, but there's a much greater impact on your income. The key question at the root of all of this is: How can you create something once to benefit thousands, if not millions, of people, without you being there?

I know I just turned on the firehose of ideas, but don't get overwhelmed. Choose one that inspires you, and build that one. It's easy to go from inspired to overwhelmed if we don't focus on one idea. I want you to stay inspired and excited, knowing this is possible for you and for your family.

If it scares you, do it, it might be a good thing to try.

— Seth Godin

"WHEN YOU LEARN
HOW MUCH YOU'RE
WORTH, YOU'LL
STOP GIVING PEOPLE
DISCOUNTS."

— KAREN SALMANSOHN

CHAPTER 6
WHY YOU NEED TO QUIT YOUR JOB AND GO INTO BUSINESS FOR YOURSELF

If you do what's easy, your life will be hard,

but if you do what's hard, your life will be easy.

— Les Brown

You might be thinking, How am I supposed to get out of debt if I quit my job?

Personally, I enjoyed my 9-to-5 job for a long time. Let me re-phrase that: I enjoyed the job and the money. I didn't enjoy the two-hour commute back and forth each day, or getting told what to do by my boss. I wasn't one of those guys who hated his job and his boss and complained every second, but I was getting bored and not feeling challenged. Maybe that's the reason you're reading this book—because you're looking for something new, or you have a dream that's bigger than working a 9-to-5 job for someone else.

The real problem with most jobs is that they pay you just enough to keep you from not quitting, but not enough to get ahead after expenses and taxes. Hence the acronym: just over broke.

With a job, there are barely any tax write-offs with the government, and when you're on salary, the government takes a piece of the pie before you get yours. In most states and provinces, you're taxed at a higher rate compared to someone who runs a business. That's because tax laws favor those who provide jobs for other people. This makes sense, because business owners are the ones taking the risk—buying equipment, renting office space, and hiring staff.

MY STORY

Despite not hating my job, I wanted more. I had a dream to share my music, so I juggled both for a while, doing the 9-to-5 and playing gigs on the weekends. Every year I'd use up all my vacation time to play shows to push my dream forward. It got to the point that I couldn't ask for any more time off.

In my book, Fighter, I shared how I went from working five days a week to asking for Fridays off—and how when my boss said yes it felt like a miracle. I eventually got up the courage to ask if I could take a leave of absence for a tour across Canada, and shortly after that, I asked if I could go down to working only three days a week. This was a pretty scary request, but again it was granted—and I was so appreciative to have more time to work on my dream.

At first, it was exciting to have those days off. But the reality was that I was my own boss four days a week, and I had to make sure I used that time to earn the money I wouldn't be getting from my job. I knew I had to book shows to get my music out there or I'd be begging my boss for those days back.

It wasn't a walk in the park, at all. Some days I'd wake up depressed, feeling the effects of the rejection emails you inevitably get when you reach out in the music business. I also had the added pressure that if I didn't sell I didn't get paid—unlike going to work where I'd get paid no matter what. In the real world of business, and especially the music industry, results are what count, not good intentions or excuses. It wasn't working out as smoothly as I hoped, but I forced myself to sit down in front of my computer and keep sending out emails. I quickly learned it was just a numbers game and about 5% of the emails I sent would lead to a sale, or in this case, a concert booking. It was the exact same process as writing this book. I didn't always feel like writing, but I disciplined myself to keep writing even through the not-so-exciting moments.

WE ARE ALL SALESPEOPLE

In those early days, a lot of artists on the outside looking in thought I just recorded songs all day and rocked out in the studio, but that couldn't have been further from the truth. I didn't run a studio and I wasn't a producer or engineer. As an artist, I recorded albums and then had to get out there and promote them to earn a living. This is where most people fail in music and in business: marketing themselves.

You don't have a business because you have a logo and business cards. You have a business when you've sold something to a customer and made money. That's when you're "in business."

If you don't work hard to make your dreams a reality, then you're going to be employed by someone to work on their dreams.

— Manafest

When I met my hero, Peter J. Daniels, for the first time, he told me if I just got my marketing right, I wouldn't be asking him my silly financial questions. It took four years before I understood what he was trying to get across to me: if you don't get good at selling, you're not going to make it.

Does the idea of selling make you uncomfortable? I hate to break it to you, but we are all salespeople.

I had to sell my wife on dating me first; then I had to sell her on staying with me and eventually marrying me. If I was rude to her early on in our relationship because I'd had a bad day at work, that wouldn't be selling her on me very well. If I had bad breath, didn't shower after skateboarding, cracked rude jokes or was late picking her up—that wouldn't sell her on me, either.

In business you are constantly selling yourself, and it goes beyond selling your product or service. If you're late for a meeting, you need to call or email ahead, or re-schedule if you have to. Stuff happens—and as long as you're respectful about it, no worries. But if you're someone who is constantly 10 or 15 minutes late, you'd better get your act together. If you make me wait 15 minutes, I'm gone, and you'll never get an appointment again. Why? Because you just wasted what's most precious to me: time.

I had a guy invite me to be on his podcast recently. I showed up five minutes early, because that's respectful. He showed up after I did, then asked me semi-interesting questions to see if I was worthy enough to be on his podcast. Wasn't that why I was there? Turned out he wanted to re-schedule for later, which wasn't going to happen because he'd wasted my time. He was super unprofessional, and he did a poor job selling himself.

I have to sell my song ideas to my producers so they'll record them. I just emailed a song to my radio team and shared a little story to sell them on promoting the song on the radio. I have to paint a picture of what it is I'm trying to sell in the best light. Some people call this pre-framing. If I tell you I'm going to see a movie, and you tell me, "It's amazing," you've pre-framed my thoughts and opinion about the movie before I've even seen it.

If you've ever watched Shark Tank—which is a great show, by the way—you know that some of the entrepreneurs walk into the tank to pitch their business idea bubbling with enthusiasm and passion. They sell their idea like crazy, and those people normally get a deal. It's the ones who don't know their product, their numbers or their business, who can't sell their idea to the sharks and get rejected.

The way you dress, the way you speak and write, and the way you present yourself in public tells the world something about you, and it's either positive or negative.

If I were to parachute into your life unannounced and look at your office, bedroom, or car, would I see an organized person or an unorganized mess?

Right now, as I'm writing this book, it's 7:30 a.m. I just flew through the night from Toronto to Germany. I spilled mango sherbet on my pullover sweater, so I changed before I got picked up by my driver. Why? Because you only get one chance at a first impression. Learn to sell. In business you're always selling to your prospects, investors, and employees.

> *To be the best salesperson, put yourself in the shoes of the person to whom you're selling. Don't sell your product. Solve their problems.*
>
> *– Mark Cuban*

FOCUS TO FINISH

When I was at my 9-to-5 job, I worked my butt off day and night! I wrote songs at 6:30 a.m. into a voice recorder as I drove to work. I didn't take lunch breaks. I worked on my music career while I ate my lunch in my office. I was working on my dream! I was reading, emailing, and making phone calls. Honestly, I probably went a little overboard on the music stuff at work, but I was so passionate. Sometimes I stayed late to work on my music, because I knew I'd just be in traffic anyway. It made sense to work on music at the office where the internet connection was fast and then get home quicker once the traffic had died down. It's called sacrifice. It's called hustle. It's called squeezing every second out of every day to make your dream work and build your new life.

I don't even think I had a plan at the time; I was just working at it because I loved it. But I was really building a business that would one day allow me to quit my 9-to-5.

That's what I want you to do: become an entrepreneur and start working for yourself. "There is no 9-to-5—there's only nine till faint," as Les Brown puts it. Life doesn't just hand you your dreams. You have to work at it and never take no for an answer. You have to keep climbing. Once I got to the point where my music supported my family, I started working on other things, like my online businesses, real estate investments and other business ventures.

What you don't want to do is scatter your energy in five different directions. You have to focus, which stands for Follow One Course Until Successful. Too many people start and stop, start and stop, and jump from one thing to the next. You don't want to be a jack of all trades but master of none. By trying to do too many things, you dilute your effectiveness in all of them. Rather than putting average effort into too many things, put a focused effort of time, energy, and thought into just a few important projects. Don't just be a starter—be a finisher. If you haven't read the book The One Thing, by Gary Keller, I highly recommend it.

Don't try to pursue every available opportunity that comes your way, because when you say yes to one thing, you're saying no to something else. Decide who you are and who you want to become— and decide what you don't want to become as well.

IF YOU CAN'T QUIT YOUR JOB YET

Often, we get too absorbed on what we are going to get from working at a job as opposed to who we are becoming by being there. When looking at a job and weighing up if it's right for you, think about both. Consider what connections, experience, and inspiration you'll gain, as well as how much you'll be paid.

A while ago, I got the opportunity to visit the Facebook headquarters in Austin, Texas. Facebook had noticed the success I was having with the ads I run on their platform and so they invited me to visit. It was an incredible experience: not only were all the different workspaces super creative and inspiring, but the cafeteria was epic. They had smoothies, fresh fruit, and a chef cooking up fresh dishes right in front of you. I thought if I were a young kid starting over again, I'd like to work there, just because the environment was so inspiring.

Some people dream of success, while others wake up and work hard at it.

– Mark Zuckerberg

START LATE BUT FINISH GREAT

Maybe you started late. That's ok. Ray Kroc, who built the McDonald's franchise, didn't have success until his mid fifties. If you read his story, Grinding It Out, you'll find he had many failures and trials trying to figure things out, but he didn't quit.

If you think working on your dream, waking up early, staying up late and giving that extra effort is hard, wait until life hands you the bill five years from now for not trying. The pain of regret is much heavier on the body and mind than the pain of daily effort. As I've gotten older, I've found it sad to see so many people who started with all these big hopes now have nothing to show for it because they gave up too soon. I challenge you to "grind it out" until your dream manifests.

PASS IT DOWN TO THE NEXT GENERATION

Another reason you need to go into business is because it will set a great example for your kids. At four years old, my daughter is starting to notice that I'm available to drive her to school and pick her up most days. She sees Daddy working whenever he feels like it. I wouldn't be able to do this if I had a boss who required me to be somewhere at 9:00 a.m.

Yes, sometimes I have to go to work at odd hours of the day or evening, but that might be down the street at Starbucks or in my home office. She knows I'm not far away and that I'm available if she needs me. She's understanding more and more about what I do, and it's not uncommon for her to ask me if I made any money today!

I want to build a business I can pass down to her. I want to pass down not only my music and the real estate I've invested in, but also the knowledge and the lessons that have enabled me and my wife to build this life we have. Melanie and I know we have a calling from God on our life to reach many people through our businesses, and one day our daughter will take our reach even further.

We're laying a foundation for the generations who'll come after us. I don't want my daughter or her kids to start from scratch trying to figure out business and finance. That's why I'm writing books, creating courses, and leaving a legacy for them to launch into at their appointed time.

How amazing would it have been if my grandfather's father had started a business that was passed down to him, and he passed it down to my father, and then my father passed it down to me? Can you imagine if they had just invested in real estate or a business that grew with each generation? It would be worth millions of dollars, and would have allowed my wife and I to stand on the shoulders of giants. God encourages us to leave an inheritance for our children's children. We are supposed to be trail blazers, leading the way, being salt and light for our next generation.

I want my daughter to start thinking like an entrepreneur before she's 10 years old, and I challenge you to teach your kids to do the same. But being successful isn't just about finance, it's about having a great idea and a worthy cause to work for. Finances help, but nothing beats passion for a worthy cause. I want to instill that benevolence in my daughter too.

Going into business not only provides wealth in the area of finances, but wealth in the form of time and family. Make it your goal to start a side business that is bigger than you are and can be passed down to future generations.

It's true that money won't buy you happiness, but it's a lot better than being broke. I'd rather be rich and unhappy then broke and unhappy—and with God's blessings, I am rich and happy.

The blessings of the Lord makes one rich,

And He adds no sorrow with it.

— Proverbs 10:22

"IF YOU DON'T WORK HARD TO MAKE YOUR DREAMS A REALITY, THEN YOU'RE GOING TO BE EMPLOYED BY SOMEONE TO WORK ON THEIR DREAMS."

— MANAFEST

CHAPTER 7

HOLY SMOKES, THAT WAS EASIER THAN I THOUGHT: SECRETS TO STARTING AN ONLINE BUSINESS

The biggest people with the biggest minds can be shot down by the smallest people with the smallest minds. Think big anyway.

– *Kent Keith*

It was 2012, and I was on the bullet train in Japan promoting my new album, Fighter, on an eight-city tour. Never wanting waiting time to be wasted time, I had my iPhone loaded with podcasts and audio books for the journey. As my mobile college played in my ears, pumping me up with ideas and inspiration, one guy's story really caught my attention.

This dude Pat Flynn, from San Diego, California, has a podcast called "Smart Passive Income." When he was in college, he'd aced an architect exam, and blogged his step-by-step study process. When he compiled this information into an e-book and charged money for it, within 24 hours he'd made a few hundred dollars in sales. In the following months, the sales rolled in and eventually he'd earned thousands—just by sharing something that he knew.

As I rode the bullet train with my bandmates, ready to rock a show, I found it baffling and at the same time massively motivating to try to understand how this guy was selling his knowledge to people online all over the world. I didn't yet know how I'd do it, but the seed of inspiration was definitely planted as I imagined what knowledge I could offer to help and even inspire people across the globe. The principle I want you to take in here is: people will pay you for what you know.

In Chapters Four and Five I touched on the billion dollar business that is online education, and this chapter is all about taking that to the next level. There are people all over the world searching Google and YouTube about all kinds of topics—and those with books, videos, and online courses covering those topics are making a fortune selling what we call "info products."

Sell your mind, not your soul.

– Valiant

DON'T DEVALUE WHAT YOU KNOW

So many of us devalue what we know because we already know it; it's second nature to us. It's like the magician who we all look up to when they wow us with their tricks, but the minute we learn their secret, we instantly dismiss and devalue the illusion because now we know how they did it. We've seen behind the curtain and the mystery is gone. (That's why magicians live by a common code never to share their secrets.) But devaluing what you know is a huge mistake, because the simple and wonderful truth is that there are people out there who will pay you for it.

Know your value so people can respect your worth.

— Unknown

In almost every city in the world, tour guides are paid to show people around the place they live in. They turn their knowledge of a specific city into a business, and tourists willingly pay for the inside take.

Interestingly, this is a model I've seen replicated online, where you can find courses on how to tour and experience theme parks like Disney World. People are happy to pay to learn all the little secrets to getting around the park quickly, because it maximizes the fun they'll have on their trip.

It's truly awesome when you share your passion and find that people are willing to pay for a piece of it. I had a taste of this when people started paying me for my music, but I couldn't fully wrap my head around this concept until I wrote my first book, Fighter: 5 Keys to Conquering Fear & Reaching Your Dreams.

The biggest motivator in getting my story out there was that I knew I wasn't the only person in the world who'd struggled with fear. While it took a dose of courage to write and publish my story, I did it knowing my book might inspire people. Fighter continues to sell thousands of copies even today, and I never get tired of hearing how it helps other people conquer their own fears and reach for their dreams.

Looking back, I can see that the next logical step from sharing my story as a book was to branch out into creating my own online courses. This is why I got so motivated whenever I heard anyone talking about the concept of people paying you for what you know: because I knew I still had more to say and share.

Along with the moment on the bullet train in Japan, there were two other pivotal moments which made me finally take the plunge and make my first course. One was when my friend Shane Sams told me there was a guy who'd created a course on raising chickens. "That's it," I said, "if these guys can do it, then so can I."

But the final push came when I was driving up I-5 in Orange County, California, after an amazing surf in San Onofre. I was listening to a podcast about online business and the topic of teaching what you know came up again.

These guys were talking about how this one dude was making thousands of dollars on a website called Udemy.com, and it was like the final piece of the puzzle had fallen into place.

I pulled over to the closest Starbucks, grabbed a London Fog, and wrote out what became one of my first outlines to teach artists and musicians how to be successful in the music business.

I was so excited to finally be taking action. Like anyone who's pursued an unusual career path I've made my share of mistakes—but after hundreds of thousands of albums sold and 22 countries toured, I've learned a lot, too.

I always get tons of questions from aspiring artists at shows, in the greenroom backstage, and via fan emails so I was genuinely eager when I discovered this new way to help people fast-track their career and become successful.

Melanie is always supportive of my crazy ideas. Even when she was seven months pregnant she helped me film my very first course in our tiny two-bedroom apartment. We set up the backdrop, lights, and video camera. She stood behind the camera ready to film me and counted me down: "Three, two, one, go!"

Standing in our living room, staring into a camera lens, I poured my heart out about everything I knew about the music business. I felt ridiculous, but I tried to focus on providing as much value as possible, thinking of my students on the other end who would one day watch it.

In between shots or when I'd screw up, I'd say to my wife, "Why am I doing this, this is so stupid, no one's gonna buy this." She kept on encouraging me, saying, "You sound amazing, keep going!"

I pushed through the self-doubt and gave the course my all. Once it was uploaded I promoted it the best I could with the little knowledge I had of marketing at the time, and—incredibly—people all over the world not only bought it but they loved it and were inspired by it. The coolest part was I was reaching people I didn't even know.

One night, driving home from a Bible study group, when I got another notification that someone had joined my course, a realization hit me: not only was this inspiring because I was helping people, but it was happening while I was doing something else. I was making a sale without having to be there.

This was my first introduction to the info product space. I didn't make thousands of dollars overnight, but I will say I've now made a total of $70,000+ on the Udemy platform alone.

Do you know the upfront costs to creating this course? A USB microphone, a built-in laptop video camera, lights, and an internet connection. That's it! There are a few more tools we use, and I made a complete gear list for you at https://www.manafest.com/gearlist

I heard a story from a famous copywriter named Ben Settle who sells info products online, including an e-book that's priced at $3.99 on Amazon. When one of Ben's friends told him he'd hired a coach for a one-on-one consulting and paid $30,000, Ben asked a few questions about what he learned during the session.

Turns out a lot of the content was the same stuff Ben teaches in his $3.99 e-book. Dang, he thought, I need to raise my prices. Like all of us, Ben devalues what he knows. We assume just because we know something, everybody else knows it too. But they don't.

KICKING SELF-DOUBT TO THE CURB

I can hear you saying, "But I'm not an expert," or "I'm not a teacher," or "I don't have a degree." I didn't think I was, either. But an expert is just someone one step further than the next guy. My daughter thinks I'm an expert at tying shoelaces because she doesn't know how to yet.

When I started to coach other music artists, I could have said, "I'm not Eminem, Linkin Park, Bruno Mars, or whoever the most current famous artist is, so what right do I have to teach someone else?" But the truth is, the majority of people looking for help are just getting started. Often they just need to get to the next step on their journey.

You don't need to have special credentials, letters after your name, or have won a ton of awards to start helping people. Don't wait for someone to certify you or knight you as worthy to teach. If you know something that can help someone, then it's your duty to start helping them.

It's common to feel doubt. Melanie didn't think she was qualified to teach—despite the fact that she's sold thousands of art prints all over the world, been featured in large retail chains across the USA, and has a very successful design business.

But in her mind, she was comparing herself to the most famous artists out there—when in reality, there are thousands of men and women who would love to be able to sell their art like she does, but don't know where to start.

As she watched me create more courses and generate more passive income for our family, she finally said, "That's it! I'm creating one too!" Her first course was on how to sell your art online and build a digital art print business, and although it made a little bit of money on Udemy the first month, Melanie still wasn't fully sold that she was doing the right thing being on there.

A short while later, I was recording my new album in Nashville, when my friend Seth Mosley told me about another online course platform called Skillshare. It looked legit, so after our studio session I spent the rest of the evening uploading my courses and Melanie's to that website.

A short while later I was back home and Melanie was in the kitchen, cooking some food, a little bummed about her courses not doing so well on Udemy. "Why don't I upload your courses to this other website called Skillshare.com? I heard from Seth it's pretty legit." She said "No!" and then we got in a fight about it because I said, "too late, I already did it," as I started to laugh.

A couple of months after uploading her courses to Skillshare she was making thousands of dollars a month. We were both freaking out at how much money she made—we couldn't believe it! Plus, it was in US dollars, which are worth more than Canadian dollars, so it had an even bigger impact on us while we were living in Canada.

Melanie now sells courses from her website at Visioncity.biz as well as other platforms like Udemy and Skillshare. She has thousands of students all over the world who love her teaching, give awesome feedback and reviews, and even recognize her in public. I laugh and say, "You're the famous one now." I'm so proud of her.

When we first got started creating online courses, we'd go for walks talking about it. I remember saying, "Wow, wouldn't it be amazing if we could make an extra $1000 a month?" Then with hard work and perseverance, it happened. The next goal was, well, what if we started making $5000 a month? And then that happened. Again, we were totally blown away by the results.

Success like this is a dream come true, especially after all those years of living on the road, thousands of miles away, trying to earn a living for our family. Now I get to work with my wife every single day, doing what we love, helping people while changing our family tree forever. If you want to do something you've never done before, you have to be someone you've never been before.

Selling stuff is easy. All you gotta do is give away stuff that makes people happy…and then sell stuff that makes 'em even happier.

— Frank Kern

Creating courses by teaching what you know is what I call the power of leverage: the idea of doing the work once but getting paid for it over and over again. Public school teachers teach 20 or 30 students at a time. But by creating an online course, you can teach thousands or even millions of people without leaving your house. There are people out there just waiting to learn something from you.

We wrote a step-by-step guide to creating your first online course, and you can download at www.manafest.com/courseguide.

Every time I chat with someone and the topic of money or freeing up their time comes up, I always ask if they are selling an online course or eBook. It has changed our life so much, I feel obligated to share it with everyone.

You will get all you want in life if you help
enough other people get what they want.
– Zig Ziglar

WHAT SHOULD YOU TEACH?

Many people get stuck at not knowing what they should teach. I say, start with something you know really well. For me, it was music, because I had so much experience in that arena. When I sat down in Starbucks that day to sketch out ideas, they just oozed out of me.

Think about what you're passionate about, and where your experience lies. What do your friends or your kids call you to get your advice on? What's the subject that makes you light up, that you love talking about?

There are people out there teaching all kinds of crazy things and making a great living doing it. As well as 'How to experience Disneyland' I mentioned a few pages ago, I've seen courses for things like:

- How to train your dog

- How to knit

- How to write a bestseller

- Learn to play the guitar

- The basics of bitcoin

- How to manage real estate

If you really want to test your idea, go to Amazon and see if any books on your topic have already been published. You can also go to Udemy or Skillshare to see if someone has created a course on the subject. And please, please, please just because someone else already created a course in your chosen area doesn't mean you can't create one, too.

In fact, that just validates your idea even more, especially if you see they've got lots of students. Their success confirms there's a need in the marketplace. Don't look to copy them, but think how you can teach this topic differently in your unique style. Your voice, story, and approach to the topic will be very different from the next person, and people like to learn from different points of view.

What I've come to realize is that people buy more than one course or book on a subject if they're really interested in it. I buy many books on leadership, finances, and music from multiple different sources, and I learn something different from each author. If you don't see a course or book on the subject you're thinking of teaching, be a little cautious, because there might not be demand for your topic.

When creating a course think about where a person is now, and where they'd like to be. Your course is their guide, helping them get there faster and easier without all the pain you went through. Don't focus solely on making money from your course. Focus on the transformation of your students.

If your motivation is to help people, the money will follow. I truly want you to have a pure heart with this and see that you can fulfill a need, help millions of people, and get paid all at the same time. Go for it!

Stop looking for all the hard ways to make a little bit of money,
and start looking at all the easy ways to make a lot of money.
— Myron Golden

"SELL YOUR MIND, NOT YOUR SOUL."

— VALIANT

CHAPTER 8

ACCELERATE YOUR SUCCESS WITH LESS STRESS AND TIME: GET A MENTOR!

A few years ago I made a 2200 mile trip from Toronto to Sedona, Phoenix, to get one-on-one coaching with a guy called Chris, a leading business mentor who ran an online group program I'd attended which specialized in Facebook ads. The program consisted of weekly video chats where we could ask questions and get hands-on advice on our businesses, but over the last three calls, nobody else showed up. This meant I got three sessions of exclusive support from Chris to coach me with my business!

Every time we spoke, he helped me out so much that I always earned more money after our conversations. Even though I was making a ton of progress, I knew I needed more coaching. So when Chris offered me a two-day one-on-one consulting package where I could fly to Sedona to work with him and his team, I knew this would be an awesome chance for me to accelerate my success even further.

One ticket from Toronto to Phoenix and $5000 later, and I'm

sitting on the plane, waiting to land, with my heart pumping—in a really good way. I was so ready to make the most of the learning opportunity I was about to embark on. One of Chris' team members picked me up from the airport in a Mercedes Benz. He had a heavy Boston accent and cursed like a sailor, but he was one of the funniest dudes I ever met. He specialized in YouTube ads, and we chatted about online business the whole drive up.

After a few hours driving north we got to Sedona, this super hipster, New Age town. As we pulled up to Chris' house, he and his new fiancé answered the door. We visited a little and then it was straight down to mapping out my business. We worked from 10:00 a.m. to 12 midnight both days, and it was one of the best investments I've ever made for my business.

There's nothing quite like having an experienced guide to help you get a different perspective. Sometimes you're just too close to your business to see the potential opportunities or pitfalls. I've paid mentors upwards of $1000 an hour, and that might sound crazy, but I always take multiple ideas from those conversations to make 10 times that amount.

INVESTING IN SUCCESS

It's always been a goal of both mine and Melanie's to continue to learn and educate ourselves as we journey through life and business together. Several years ago we invested $18,000 to fly to a four-day intensive to learn from the brightest minds in online business. That was an important moment for us: it was the moment we went all in. We were so committed. I'm not saying you have to spend that much money to get started with your business, but by this point we had solid ambitions to build and develop our online brands, and we knew we needed expert-level guidance to get closer to where we wanted to be. Let me just say the money we invested came back ten-fold.

A few years ago I came to understand that until I was willing to invest thousands in my education, I wouldn't have the belief in myself to charge thousands to other people. You have to make the deposit before you can request a return.

Even today, I seek advice from people who've made millions in order to get the perspective I need to fast-track my success even further. Within minutes, they can identify problems in my business, plug up holes, and suggest ideas I've never considered. I can't tell you how many thousands of dollars I've missed out on just because I was missing a vital piece of information—but the fact is—you don't know what you don't know.

> *One of the greatest values of mentors*
> *is the ability to see ahead to what others cannot see*
> *and help them navigate a course to their destination.*
> *– John C. Maxwell*

CUT YOUR LEARNING CURVE IN HALF

I've always found working with a great coach to be such a powerful process, and a real shortcut for success. But I get that as you read this, you might not be in a position—yet—to invest big sums of money into a coaching or mentoring program.

Maybe you're like me at the start of my journey, with no business education, wealth, or role models in your immediate circle. If that's the case then your first stop to accessing mentor support is to pick up a book (or two, or ten) by someone who's been there, done that. I love to read rags-to-riches stories by successful men and women.

I know I've already beaten the drum for the power of reading in this book but for a good reason! It is hands-down one of the most accessible and cost-effective ways to educate yourself. Success leaves clues, and you'll find so many hidden inside the pages of books. Why wouldn't you pay $20 for a book that can give you information someone spent 20 years learning and cut your learning curve in half?

Another option is to attend live events in the field you want to excel at. Just by being in a room with like-minded individuals taps you into the natural synergy you get from being surrounded by motivated and aspirational people. There are tons of free and paid live events out there where the speakers will provide invaluable first-hand information. Most events also present the opportunity to network so you can build long-term relationships with people who will impact your mindset as well as your bank account.

The first live event I attended was called Experts Academy in California hosted by best-selling author Brendon Burchard. I'd picked up his book Millionaire Messenger while on tour in a thrift shop for 50 cents and devoured it in a few days, but I wanted more so I started watching his videos on YouTube. Then I still wanted more so that's when I invested in one of his online courses which came with two tickets to his live seminar. The second ticket I gave to a friend who recently told me this was a pivotal moment in his life, and he is forever grateful for the opportunity to go. I know for a fact this is true because I've seen the difference it's made in his life and his family's.

Also look out for online coaches with special offers as an incentive to sign up for their email newsletter—you might get a free spot on a webinar or access to an e-book that will help get you inspired. Though it isn't the same as laser-focused advice you get one-on-one, it's a good way to get an idea of what potential coaches are offering, and when you start earning more maybe you'll look that coach up and book a tailored one-on-one session.

In essence, a mentor is someone you can trust to have your best interests in mind, without any agenda except to see you succeed. Their fulfillment comes from seeing you rise to the challenge and achieve success. A mentor is there to encourage and support you. They are not there to babysit you or do the work for you, but they're a coach in your corner, cheering you on and keeping you accountable by holding your feet to the fire. You have to do the work, but we all need a guide to help us stay focused and have perspective. Personally, I love it when a mentor tells me off. It challenges me to think, dream, and act bigger.

What got you here won't get you there.

— Marshall Goldsmith

QUALIFY YOUR MENTORS

Remember the music manager I told you about in Chapter Two who squashed my ambitions and gave me absolutely no useful advice at all? Yeah, I really should have done a little research on that guy before I hired him. One of the fastest ways to qualify your mentors is by seeing if this person has achieved what you want to achieve. Does this potential mentor bear the fruit in his or her life that you are trying to grow and harvest in yours?

With a little research, you can see if they've got the goods to back up their claims. This can be seen in video testimonials, references, blog articles, reviews, magazine features—but most of all, in their reputation. A few Google searches and a couple phone calls should help gauge the person's character.

A good tree produces good fruit, and a bad tree produces bad fruit.
— Matthew 7:17

Before I ever hire someone at a higher ticket price, I've read their books, attended their seminar, or worked with them in some other capacity that got me results already. All I'm really doing is diving deeper and asking for more personal attention to my business.

I won't receive financial advice from someone who's poorer than me, just like I won't take marriage advice from someone who's divorced, or tips on dieting from an overweight person. I'm not trying to be rude, but if they don't have the results in their own life, how can they be giving advice to me? You've got to be that example.

DON'T LEARN THE HARD WAY

You don't have to learn the hard way. If someone is where you want to be, or has helped other people get to where you want to be, doesn't it make sense to pay them to tell you exactly what to do? What's funny is sometimes we know what to do, but we need someone to keep us accountable and on track. My wife and I always offer each other advice but occasionally we have trouble hearing it, and it's not until we hear it from a third party that it sinks in. I'll say, "didn't I suggest that a week ago?" and she'll reply, "yeah, but I guess I needed to hear from a different angle." I laugh because I've been guilty of the same thing.

Athletes hire workout and performance coaches. Singers hire vocal coaches and trainers. If you look at anyone super successful in their field of choice, they always have someone (or several someones) to give them that edge and keep them sharp.

GIVING BACK

Let no debt remain outstanding, except the continuing debt to love one another,

for whoever loves others has fulfilled the law.

— Romans 13:8

Since I have achieved success, I feel it is my duty to give back. In the 18 years I've spent in the music business I've learned a lot, so I've written books and created courses to help artists and musicians avoid my mistakes and fast-track their own success. Something I love about Fanbase University, my monthly group coaching program, is the group environment. Everyone benefits from the questions asked and answered, and I get to impact multiple people at the same time. It also brings serious artists together to network and support each other.

I didn't get here alone. I used to mistake wisdom with age, but now I know there are a lot of immature, unwise grown men. Yes, they've aged, but they stopped being students and they've finished growing and developing. Never stop growing. Never stop being willing to be taught something new. I am always a student before I'm a teacher.

I'll be hiring coaches and mentors when I'm 75 years old. By that point, I won't be surprised if the mentors I hire are younger then me, teaching me whatever the latest technologies are. It's not about age, but about who has the wisdom, experience, and knowledge you're looking for. Old age doesn't guarantee wisdom and youth shouldn't presume ignorance.

A wise man will hear and increase in learning,

and a man of understanding will acquire wise counsel.

— Proverbs 1:5

"WHAT GOT YOU HERE, WON'T GET YOU THERE."

— MARSHALL GOLDSMITH

CHAPTER 9
THRIVING IN THE BLACK

What happens when you've done the hard work and you're out of the red? First off, congratulations! You are a happier, healthier, more creative person. It's possible you have created wealth not just for you, but also for your loved ones. Now, the question from here is: how do you thrive in the black?

HAVE A VISION FOR YOUR LIFE

"You see that girl over there, bro? I'm going to get with that girl." This was me, speaking to a friend as we stood in front of Queen's University in Kingston, Ontario, during a Christian youth convention. This was me calling my shot before I even knew who that beautiful caramel-skinned girl with long curly brown hair was. Despite many people thinking she was way out of my league, and before I could talk myself out of approaching her, I headed over and introduced myself. We hit it off instantly, dated for five years, and have been married for over 17.

Like we discussed in Chapter One, there is something powerful when you have a vision for your life and when you're 100% sure of what you want. There is clarity in the simplicity of focusing on one thing. Don't let anyone's opinion of you stop you from pursuing the love of your life—or wealth for you and your family. And don't let anyone talk you out of your dreams just because they've given up theirs. You find this a lot when it comes to people's attitudes and ambition (or lack of ambition) towards money. Someone once told my wife she'd always be in debt—but that didn't stop her from paying off the car, her credit cards, and then the mortgage on our house.

Here's where vision comes in: you have to see yourself debt free and wealthy in your mind first. It may start out as an impossible dream, but just as I talk about in my book, Fighter, you can make that dream more tangible and real by writing that dream down. That's how it becomes a clear vision. You have a destination in mind and now you can plot your course. And while a change in thinking and mindset is crucial—it's not just a case of think and grow rich. You must think, act, and then grow rich.

What I'm asking you to do is to call your shot. Speak it in your mind and then out loud: I am committed to getting out of debt and building wealth for me and my family. Write it down, say it out loud, and hold the vision.

No matter how small you start, start something that matters.

— Brendon Burchard

CHOOSE YOUR FINANCIAL VEHICLE

Here's a question for you: how quickly do you want to get to your ideal financial destination? Are you happy to reach it in 20 years, or would you prefer to take a shortcut?

If you want to not only survive but thrive in the black I recommend you take a moment to consider that there are different routes towards your financial goal, and some will get you there faster than others. The difference is the vehicle you use to get to where you want to be.

When I was a teenager, I would sometimes walk to my high school and it would take me 45 minutes. If I ran, it would take me 30 minutes. If I skateboarded, I could do it in 20, and if my mom drove me, I would get there in five! Just like there were different vehicles to get me to school, there are many different vehicles to get you to your financial destination.

If you believe money is an abundant resource it becomes one.

If you think it's a scarce resource it is one.

– Ian Stanley

We live in an incredible age of opportunity. The internet alone has made it possible for entrepreneurs all over the world to cut the time it took them to reach financial freedom in half—at least.

I recently watched a video where an entrepreneur named Dan Henry hit one million dollars in a day by selling 34 $30,000 coaching packages. You read that right, one million dollars in one single day. I've been in the room at seminars where the speaker pitches a coaching program in the range of $10,000 to $35,000, but Dan did this all online which makes it extra mind blowing.

Because of COVID he ran a two day seminar online providing massive value for free, and then at the end he gave people the opportunity to invest in themselves further. What's really interesting is that the opportunity was always there, but the virus and unexpected circumstances forced him to try something new. It's when we are backed into a corner with no other options that we find our true potential and what we are actually made of.

If you want to thrive in the black, stay out of debt, and build wealth for your family, I suggest you choose a business—a vehicle—that can get you there in a shorter period of time.

Here's a story that illustrates this well. Imagine two guys in the business of selling a water filter system that's easy to use: you just attach it to your faucet at home and it gives you amazing, clean, great-tasting water. One guy goes door to door selling his product to people one at a time. He's convincing and he delivers a great pitch, so he makes pretty good sales. But because some people aren't home, and there are only so many hours in a day, he can get around 20 sales per day max.

However, the other guy takes the same product, films an amazing how-to video that sells the product, and creates another video to run as an advertisement on YouTube and Facebook. When people click on his video, it takes them to a sales page on his website or Amazon, and he starts selling over 200 water filters a day.

He sells way more because he is virtually knocking on 10 times the number of doors. Plus, once the ad is running, his work is done—he can focus on fulfilling product orders and growing the business.

It's not just about being in a profitable business vehicle,

but working smart inside of that vehicle.

— Manafest

MO' MONEY, MO' PROBLEMS

Money is not the root of all evil, but money will not make you happy, either. And ironically, having money can bring a new set of challenges and issues. Often these issues are rooted in fear, and it's not uncommon for newly wealthy people to get anxious about losing everything they've worked so hard to acquire.

It's like the more money we come across, the more problems we see.

— Notorious B.I.G.

Likewise, they might not realize the importance of receiving the right kind of advice and guidance required to manage wealth. The truth is, as your income continues to grow so should your circle of trusted advisors. I've had to let go of people who could no longer advise me because I was now on another playing field they no longer understood.

As your wealth increases, recognize that you now have the money to hire the right people or team of people to support you fully. You don't have to overcome your problems alone.

Something else to be aware of once you get wealthy is that you might start thinking everything you touch now turns to gold. Don't fall into the trap of investing in areas of business you know nothing about, just because you can. That's like me thinking just because I've been successful with music, I can now invest it all into stocks, which I have zero knowledge about. It's very easy to think you have the Midas touch only to squander your wealth with a few bad decisions.

It's so sad to see and hear about people who work hard to become financially free then fall prey to the pitfalls of wealth, either because they're preoccupied with the fear of losing it, or because they've cut themselves off from getting good advice and growing into their new lifestyle. That's why the Bible warns about the deceitfulness of riches. As you get the money, don't let the money get you. Have fun, make it a game, and if you're worried about money getting you, just keep loving people with it by giving it away.

However, don't think you can help people without first helping yourself. You must get before you can give. If you want to give a lot, go make a lot.

"We have a problem."

"Congratulations."

"But it's a tough problem."

"Then double congratulations."

— W. Clement Stone

At this point in my life, I've met enough of my financial goals to understand the best part about achieving any goal is the journey and the person you become in the process: the fight, the learning, and the challenge of trying to figure it out until you strike gold. While there's a lot of satisfaction that comes from reaching a financial goal, I find that moment only brings short-term happiness. God designed us to want to grow and excel beyond our current capabilities, but we also need to choose to be content while striving for the next level. As you climb the next mountain, pause and take in the scenery.

The greatest reward in becoming a millionaire
is not the amount of money that you earn.
It is the kind of person that you have to become
to become a millionaire in the first place.
— Jim Rohn

KEEP TAKING PRUDENT RISKS

You might think the words 'prudent' and 'risk' don't naturally go together, but when you consider the word prudent means to act with or show care, you might see what I'm getting at: we're talking about the risks you take and choices you make for your future—so showing care makes sense because you're the one who has to live in that future.

I've taken a lot of risks over the course of my life and career, and I'm the first to admit not all of them were prudent. I told the story earlier in the book about the biggest risk I've ever taken when I quit my job to pursue music full-time. It was the scariest, most exhilarating time of my life.

Like I said, if I could go back I'd still quit my job; I'd just wait a bit longer, because it wasn't prudent. I hadn't thought it all out properly and I could have had a much smoother transition without going through as much pain as I did. I didn't measure, I didn't sharpen my axe—I just closed my eyes and jumped in blind faith.

The second biggest risk was when Melanie and I moved to California with no job or safety net, leaving everything behind. There's something to say about the legend of Cortez here, who told his army to burn the boats while invading a new country, shouting, "No Plan B!" Sometimes you have to leave the past behind and put yourself in a "fly or die" situation. I promise it will show you what you're made of really quickly.

You better lose yourself in the music, the moment
You own it, you better never let it go
You only get one shot, do not miss your chance to blow
This opportunity comes once in a lifetime.

– Eminem

As you continue to take risks as an entrepreneur, both your stomach and bank account will drop sometimes. You've got to be able to take risks with your time, money, and energy, and expect to take a few risks before you get your reward.

As I write this part of the book, I'm 39 years old, about to turn 40. With the gift of hindsight, I can look back on my life and alongside reflecting on the crazy risks I can also see the opportunities missed.

I think of certain real estate deals, record contracts, and touring opportunities that I would have taken if I had all the information I have now. There's no point in beating myself up for a past choice, but what I can do instead is remind myself that more opportunities will come. I can shake off any feelings of regret and think about the 60-year-old version of myself who's reminding me I'd better keep taking risks and stretching for greatness.

There's no point in thinking small. It was Donald Trump who said, "If you're going to do anything, do it big." Before taking a big risk in business do your research, ask questions, email wise friends for their experienced advice, and take your emotions out of it. Then take your first step, and don't look back. Think big, dream big, and act big.

I was 66 years old. I still had to make a living. I looked at my social security check of $105 dollars and decided to use it to franchise my chicken recipe.
Folks have always liked my chicken.
– Colonel Sanders, Founder of Kentucky Fried Chicken

FINANCIAL RESERVES

"Just keep going. We've got more than enough gas," I said to the driver. We were driving through white tundra and trees after playing a concert in Yellow Knife in the North Western part of Canada. Only 45 minutes prior, a bandmate had asked me if we should fill up on gas, and I enthusiastically said, "No, we'll be fine."

An hour later, reading a business book in the back seat, I felt the minivan come to a halt. I thought to myself, "No way. Chris, you are such an idiot." We were literally in the middle of nowhere. Lifting my nose from my book, I looked around outside, and all I saw was the snow-covered road and trees. Thank God, there was a farm just up the road, and a guy from the farm filled the van up. Within 30 minutes we were back on the road, laughing. I knew we should have played it safe and filled up, but I ignored wisdom because I was in a rush to get home.

I see a version of that story so often with entrepreneurs who feel like they need to rush to get more investment properties, grow their business, and borrow like crazy. They start making decisions to keep up with Joneses. They don't keep proper reserves.

Not only can maxing yourself out make you vulnerable during a downtime in the market or industry, but you also miss out on some of the greatest of opportunities. I've heard many successful entrepreneurs say, "Never let a good crisis go to waste." What they're talking about is taking advantage of sales and discounts on properties and businesses during a downturn. That's when some of the greatest wealth transfers take place.

Prepare. Have reserves, not only for the rainy days, but so you can take part in the days of great opportunity.

My wife has always been a conservative voice, softly asking me, "What's the rush?" We always laugh about a time I took her on a sea-doo, a little self-propelled watercraft, in the ocean off Dana Point, California. I was always trying to speed up, while she was shouting, "Slow down!" and holding on for dear life.

Even though you want to push ahead as hard as you can, sometimes it's better to go a little slower so you can go faster and have a surplus of energy as well as cash. If you want to thrive in the black, you've got to learn to save and have financial reserves for those rainy days and unexpected events.

It's not sexy having money just sitting there doing nothing when you know it could be working for you, but trust me, you'll want to have some cash on hand for those turbulent times.

GOD'S MONEY

Abram was very rich in livestock, in silver, and in gold.

— Genesis 13:2

When there is an abundance of something, it becomes less valuable. When something starts to become scarce, the value goes up. Everybody is drinking calmly at the bar until they hear the last call to get a drink—then the rush happens. Kanye West knows this all too well; when the supply of Yeezy shoes is limited, he is able to charge high prices.

Every day, the money in your bank account becomes less and less valuable because the government keeps printing it. Every day your dollars have less and less purchasing power because the government won't stop creating money and going into more debt. Prior to August 15th, 1971 the US government wasn't able to print money like it does today because the US dollar was still partly backed by gold. Believe it or not, before 1971 you could exchange your US or Canadian dollars at the bank for gold and silver. Then the centralized banking system was adopted and the link between the dollar and gold was fully severed.

This essentially allowed the banks and the government to devalue the purchasing power of our currency which diminished monetary wealth from its citizens. This is why the cost of goods keep rising and why your parents' house is able to sell for 10 times more than what they purchased it for. It's not that the goods you buy at the grocery or department store are worth more, it's that our money has less purchasing power.

One way to protect yourself from this is by investing in tangible assets such as properties, land and precious metals. Gold is God's currency, and it's our God-given right to own it. When the next depression hits, you'll be at a major disadvantage if you don't have at least 20% of your total assets in gold and silver.

You should also have cash on hand that is easily accessible but not necessarily in the bank. Gold and silver have stood the test of time as a form of exchange for thousands of years, while different currencies come and go. Precious metals hold intrinsic value, speak all languages, and are accepted globally.

Our paper money only carries worth while a government's creditability holds strong. Because it's no longer backed by gold or silver, our currency is a fiat currency: worthless paper that has been given value from its government but holds no intrinsic value in itself.

In 1922, Germany experienced hyperinflation because their government continued to print unbacked fiat currency. There's an article on Mashable.com that tells the extent of the crisis, reporting on how "Workers brought wheelbarrows, sacks and suitcases to work to collect their wages.

According to one story, a distracted worker found that his suitcase was stolen, with his wages dumped out and left behind." Kids were cutting up real money like it was monopoly money and using it for kindling. Some shop owners returned to a bartering system, offering goods and repairs in exchange for food.

History is repeating itself now as our governments in the western world create billions of dollars out of thin air with nothing to back it. But you cannot dig your way out of a hole.

Privately minted gold or silver coins can be used anywhere in the world, and will be accepted as a form of exchange without hesitation because of their intrinsic value.

You might be wondering how you'd sell gold or silver in the case of an economic downturn or disaster. Look around any mall or main street and it won't be long before you see huge signs that say, "We buy gold." The question is, what do these businesses know about gold that we don't, and what have we been manipulated to believe?

If you do buy gold or silver coins, make sure they are privately minted coins with some religious significance attached to them in case the government signs an executive order to recall all the gold back from its citizens like it did in 1933. If you buy government-issued coins, you are never the owner, only the bearer; the government could call back those coins at any time but they are less likely to if they are classified as unusual or hold religious significance. This topic is way too deep for this book, but for further study on precious metals, go to Danel.ch.

Gold is the money of kings, silver is the money of gentlemen,

barter is the money of peasants—but debt is the money of slaves.

— Norm Franz

PROTECTING YOUR WEALTH

Once you have wealth, it's your job to protect that wealth and secure it for the next generation. One of the best means of doing this is through a trust. I learned about trusts from my mentor Graham Daniels, from Adelaide, Australia, who focuses on asset protection strategies for businesses and families. Prudent wealthy people put their assets, including real estate and intellectual property, in trusts to prevent from unruly confiscation.

INTERNATIONAL DIVERSIFICATION

Another strategy that I learned from Graham Daniels was international diversification. It's common to hear about diversifying your assets into precious metals, real estate, and other types of wealth, but what about having some of your assets protected in a jurisdiction outside the country you live in? If we look through the pages of history, we quickly see that empires rise and fall.

A good man leaves an inheritance to his children's children...

— Proverbs 13:22

Having assets like gold, silver, or real estate owned offshore in another country is wise. I'm not talking about hiding money or doing anything illegal; I'm talking about storing your assets in more than one country. Just like you shouldn't have all your assets tied to one bank, why have all your wealth tied to one country?

I once had a bank accuse me of fraud. They shut down all my accounts with no warning for 30 days, and I couldn't access money to pay my bills. It was very scary and a huge wake-up call that once you put your money in the bank, you don't own it anymore. If you don't believe me, try going to your bank and withdrawing more than $10,000 in cash. You'll be subject to scrutiny and you'll be asked a lot of questions.

If the tension in a country gets out of control, having an exit strategy for you and your family is very wise. I'm not trying to scare you, but in my opinion we live in one of the most turbulent geo-political times in all of history.

How is one to know what one can accomplish until he tries.

— OG Mandino

BANKING IS A BUSINESS NOT A CHARITY

One day, my bank manager left me a voicemail that ended, "Thank you for your business."

Never forget that banks are not there to be your friends; they are there to be in business. Their business model is designed to keep you enslaved to debt for the rest of your life if they can. I'm not talking about the friendly bank tellers, or even my bank manager. I'm talking about the banking system.

Isn't it amazing that we put our money in the bank, and they give us 0-3% interest on it, but then they lend us the same money back in the form of mortgages and credit cards with interest rates of 4% to 24%? Once you deposit your money, they loan it at a much higher interest rate than they're paying you.

If you don't have a financial education and start playing the bank game, you're always going to be broke. Your money should never just sit around in the bank doing nothing. You should always have a plan for your money.

My wife and I have a policy that whenever we have a certain amount in our bank account, it's time to move some of it. Either we invest in real estate or our business, or we pay down one of our properties. I don't care if it's an extra $5,000 that I put down on a property that pays me 4% back; I'd rather that than leave it sitting in the bank getting 0% interest. If your money isn't working for you, then it's working for someone else.

STAY SURROUNDED BY GOOD PEOPLE

One of the key ingredients that really allowed me to thrive in the black was making the conscious choice to hang around big thinkers. I knew I needed to surround myself with positive people who weren't afraid to dream big and who could answer my tough questions and challenge me. Most of all, I wanted their good habits to rub off on me. It's so useful to have guidance from someone who's already trodden the path as you take your first steps down it.

As you read and implement the tools in this book and others like it, you might have the impulse to tell all your current friends what you're learning about money. As you earn more, you might want to help others out—and while that's commendable, don't forget your #1 goal should be to get yourself and family right first, so then you can be in a better position to help others.

Also be aware that if you do lend a hand to others, you may get it slapped, because some people just don't want to change. If you can't lift someone out of their pit, for your family's sake, don't let them pull you down with them.

Depending on what type of circles you move in, there are going to be many voices telling you you're crazy to consider becoming debt-free or wealthy. That's why, as my wife and I transitioned towards financial freedom, we continued to read books and listen to the messages of people who had accomplished great things.

We were building up the affirmation that we could do it and surrounding ourselves with like-minded people and high achievers. Instead of following the crowd and shrinking back, we chose to stretch.

We'd look at debt-free and wealthy people and instead of feeling like what they'd achieved was beyond us, we thought, "We're next!"—and eventually, we were.

It took time, sweat, energy, money, and many tears, but it happened. And I'm here to tell you, if you'll write down your dream, set a goal, and build a bigger vision of your life, God can do miracles. What's impossible with man is possible with God! I believe that not just for me—I believe it for you. The question is, will you believe it for yourself and your family, and then do something about it?

You have to decide what your future is going to look like, and decide right now in your heart what you want.

At the beginning of this book I suggested sharing this journey with your spouse or a loved one, and if that wasn't something you felt you could do back then I hope you'll consider it now. Give them this book to read, or get the audio version if that's more their thing. But choose your moment.

Don't just dump all over them late at night when they're exhausted from the day and try to convince them of this new plan. Instead, schedule a time over their favorite food or drink, and say you want to discuss something really important. Then begin to share from the heart, telling them why you want to do this. Paint the vision you see for your family.

Whenever I have a new crazy idea I want to share with Melanie, I understand timing is everything. I've learned to pre-frame my ideas in a clear, concise way so the chances of her understanding and saying YES are higher.

I have to really show the heart, the why, and the future if I want her to buy into a new venture—because as an entrepreneur, I have a lot of ideas and plans and (sometimes!) wild ambitions. But remember— we're all salespeople, and if you want to sell your significant other on a new idea as crazy as getting out of debt and becoming wealthy, you have to plan accordingly on how you will share your new dream.

FROM RED TO BLACK

I want this book to teach you to stop working for money and have your money start working for you. When your money starts working for you while you sleep or are on vacation, that gives you freedom— and isn't that what we all crave?

I'm tired of poverty mentality. When people say, "I don't need much, just enough to pay my bills and put food on the table," this may sound very pious or humble, but on further investigation I can't help but think it's selfish. As humans, we are all connected to each other. When we have the opportunity to help our fellow human, we should take it. If focusing on only your own bills is all you are prepared to think about, how can you contribute to the lives and wellbeing of others?

What if you allowed yourself to paint and create a bigger vision for your life, one that goes beyond meeting your own needs? I challenge you to dream bigger so you can be a blessing to others.

Money is a tool for making freedom. If Melanie and I could learn about finance, how to get out of debt, start building generational financial security, and enjoy the freedom to give to others and spend our time as we choose, so can you. Why wouldn't you be called to a life of wealth?

"HOW IS ONE TO KNOW WHAT ONE CAN ACCOMPLISH UNTIL HE TRIES."

— OG MANDINO

ABOUT THE AUTHOR

Chris Greenwood, A.K.A Manafest, is a Top 40 Billboard charting rock and hip hop artist, author, and entrepreneur. He has sold his music to millions of fans worldwide, and is an internationally known success coach, song writer, and founder of multiple successful companies.

In his bestselling debut book, Fighter, Chris shared how he overcame the loss of his father to suicide at five years old and went on to inspire a generation through music, speaking and concerts. A big believer in passing the ladder back down, Chris' latest book From Red To Black is his blueprint for financial freedom: a manual in which he shares the principles he used to break the cycle of debt and build a legacy of wealth.

Chris has been married to his teenage sweetheart Melanie for over 17 years, and together they've created a lucrative business empire blending passion with work. They live near Toronto with their young daughter, where they continue to inspire people the world over to chase their God given dreams.

OTHER BOOK BY THE AUTHOR

TO ORDER VISIT FIGHTERBOOK.NET

Fighter, 5 Keys To Conquering Fear and Reaching Your Dreams is the story of how Chris conquered his fears and found success in five stages, which he calls the anatomy of a fighter — Courage, Perseverance, Mindset, Discipline, and Willpower — the five resources we can all draw on in order to reach our dreams, no matter what they are.